Christopher Deliso

The use of
on the cov
were the m
not reflect

Author of "Hidden Macedonia"

Christopher Deliso

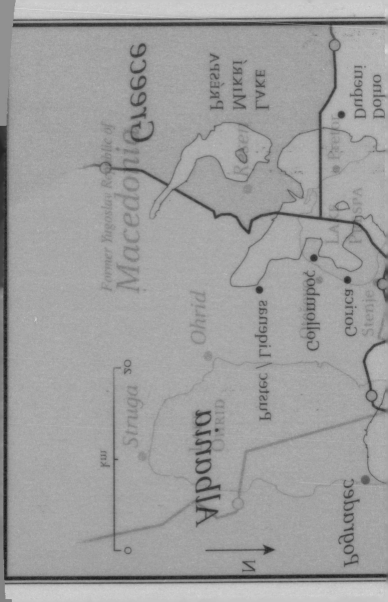

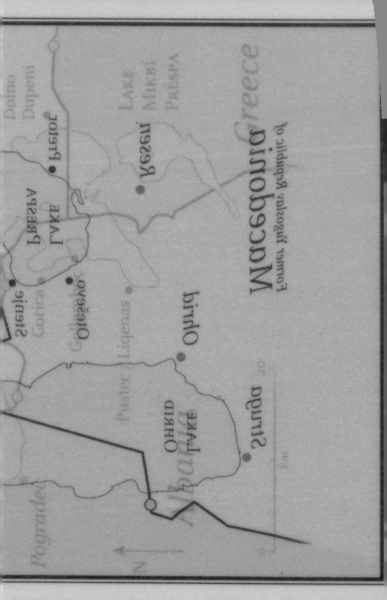

Hidden Macedonia

Hidden Macedonia

The Mystic Lakes of Ohrid and Prespa

by
Christopher Deliso

 ArmchairTraveller

HAUS PUBLISHING
London

Copyright © 2007 Christopher Deliso

First published in Great Britain in 2007 by Haus Publishing
Limited, 26 Cadogan Court, Draycott Avenue, London SW3 3BX

www.hauspublishing.co.uk

The moral rights of the author have been asserted.

A CIP catalogue record for this book is available from the British
Library

ISBN 978-1-905791-04-0

Typeset in Garamond 3 by MacGuru Ltd
Printed in Spain by Estudios Gráficos ZURE
Jacket illustration copyright © Christopher Deliso
Map reproduced by kind permission of *hidden europe* magazine:
www.hiddeneurope.co.uk

Preface

As a travel writer, there are many things I could now tell you about the great lakes region of Macedonia; how Ohrid and Prespa are among the oldest and most unique bodies of fresh water anywhere in the world, about the bewilderingly rich history that has shaped the area, about the tastes and sights and sounds that go into making it what it is.

However, since today I am feeling like the more ordinary kind of writer, and since I hope that I have managed to convey some sense of all these things in the chapters which follow, for now I won't go on about the hidden mountain villages, or the crystal-clear waters or the majestic flocks of birds, nor the scrumptious fish of Macedonia's lakes, and the ancient treasures that have been preserved in their midst. And I certainly won't be telling you that it's a real crime you haven't been there already, or to get there while you can, etc.

As an ordinary writer, there are different things I could tell you, but feeling impatient on the reader's behalf, and wanting to get started on the road to the lakes of Macedonia, I will have to leave most of them out too. So I won't go on about the lakes' complementary, yet opposed spirits, or about the infinite revelations that can be had in this ethereal borderland of blue sky, blue water and mountain ridges, all mirroring one another and history and life in countless untold ways. There is time for all that later.

For now let me just say that travelling to the lakes of Macedonia is a recurring experience, or at least one that has no definite end, and it is for this reason I have discerned, perhaps mistakenly, a certain fated quality to the lakes. Among the more tangible examples I can give of this recurrence: the other day, I was walking down the street in Skopje and there was a dusty shop window where someone else's old trophies lay ignored; the first one I saw was a tankard engraved with the name of the runner-up in a Lake Prespa fishing contest held in 1976. A few days later, again in Skopje, in an underpass where a bakery was just opening at four o'clock in the morning, a small poster on the wall celebrated the victory in the mayoral elections of the man who had been meant to meet us in Albanian Prespa, but who had unfortunately not got there in time. And just today there was Pasko Kuzman, the archaeologist, whom I bumped into as he was supervising the placing of ancient marble statues on the steps of the Macedonian government building.

This reminds me that I had better get on and thank those who helped in this endeavour, and Pasko, with his infectious laugh and clear love of his work, is certainly one of them. He made a special effort to show us the treasures of the Ohrid Museum, even thought it was well after normal opening hours. I would also like to thank Kiril Jonovski, the historian of Pretor, for graciously sharing his time and his stories with us. Jelena and her family were great hosts in Dolno Dupeni, as were Lile and her family in Vevchani. Edmond Temelko helped us vicariously in Albania, though we sadly could not stick around long enough to meet him. The Marlboro Man and his niece Natasha were excellent company on the third-to last day of the trip in Stenje, where I could also thank a cranky bull for providing colour.

And then there is George, without whom this book and this adventure would have been found wanting in many respects. His learned observations, manic driving and great all-around companionship added inestimably to the experience and thus the narrative. I also want to thank Neni, forced by circumstances to be with us for far too short a time, for adding good cheer and insights to the beginning of the journey.

My wife Buba and son Marco brought a wholly different and wonderful dimension to the adventure and created the opportunity for entirely new experiences, which I will always treasure and hold close to my heart. The support and help of my mother were essential in creating this book, and it is dedicated to her.

Finally, a note on pronunciation. Readers not familiar with the Macedonian language should note a few simple rules that take effect when the Macedonian Cyrillic alphabet is transliterated into the Latin alphabet. The most important are that 'j' is always pronounced as 'y', and that 'c' can be pronounced either as 'ts' or as 'ch'. Thus 'Trpejca' is pronounced as literally 'Terpay-tsa', while 'Pustec' is pronounced as 'Pustets', and 'Nivici' as 'Nivitsi'.

This transliterative abstruseness is also why words can have multiple spellings ('Vevcani' and 'Vevchani' are both used, though the latter alone captures the phonetic pronunciation). The transliterated letter 's' is pronounced both as a simple 's' but also moonlights as 'sh', as in 'Pestani', correctly pronounced, 'Peshtani'. Again, both spellings can be found and I hope the reader can forgive the author for replicating this inconsistency from time to time in the current book.

As for the Cyrillic 'x', that is usually transcribed with a Latin 'h' and is always pronounced like the 'ch' in 'loch', meaning that you should not feel guilty when prouncing 'Ohrid' a bit breathily.

Christopher Deliso
Skopje, Macedonia
March 2007

Hidden Macedonia

Chapter 1

There was ash on the sea at Sithonia and we were having coffee with Frede, the famous German philosopher. Fire driven by intense winds had devastated Kassandra the week before, a catastrophe for the final weeks of the tourist season, and the soot remained even in the sheltered waters between Halkidiki's first two peninsulas. It was better not to swim, but I did. Afterwards, the German, George, Neni and I spoke of Macedonia on the café patio above the beach, a soft evening breeze conveying Greek music from somewhere else.

I was planning a circular trip around the lakes of Macedonia, Prespa and Ohrid and Prespa again, taking us through three countries, and to write about it. Frede said that the book would certainly be interesting, though he never read such works. He did not have time, now that the gates of time had been opened wide to him. It is often only in retirement that people get down to their real work, and Frede was no exception. Although he had traded in his Oxford professorship, he still continued to do thinking that was really commendable and difficult in a residence on Athens' famed *Odos Theorias*, literally, the 'Street of Contemplation'. The setting it provided for Platonic and Peripatetic excess was undeniable, but preserving this did require a certain bibliographical vigilance. The house in the little Halkidiki tourist village was an acceptably ephemeral distraction for the summer, but travelogues were not, no matter what the season.

George was a former protégé of Frede's and now a fully-fledged philosophy professor himself, in Crete. I had first met him and the other Greeks at Oxford and ever since then there had been no friend as helpful as he. I had been studying Byzantine philosophy, translating unbelievably stilted Greek texts, and rather poorly too. Things were looking ominous for my degree until his providential appearance in late 1998 but after that there was no need to worry. George was the most big-hearted person I knew, not only with me but with all his friends, and his mind was a formidable repository of knowledge covering just about everything the Western humanistic tradition, and especially the Greek, had ever come up with. He was one of the last of the Renaissance men of wide learning, I thought, though such terminal despair has probably registered sometime during every generation.

Stirring what I believe was a Nescafe frappé was Neni, George's girlfriend, a dedicated psychologist, magnetic and slender and unerringly empathetic. She came from Arta, far to the west in Epiros, near Preveza and the Ionian Sea, but lived in Thessaloniki. She wanted to come with us to the lakes, but this would be decided after dinner. She had work on Monday morning. Neni's job, which involved monitoring the psychology of special-needs children, was demanding and draining and I hoped she might be able to join us, if only for a short break.

When we had finished our coffee and George had gotten the latest from his mentor, the old philosopher left us. 'Enjoy your trip, and the best of luck with your book,' he said with a wave. 'He was very nice,' said Neni. 'And a really great thinker,' pronounced George.

Dusk was falling over the ashen sea and we left. We made it full-throttle back to Thessaloniki in just over an hour, spirited there by George and his new car. It was a Volkswagen and he had bought it after trading in his old one, a Renault, to an Orthodox priest. It was a very good car and well suited for the trip ahead.

Thessaloniki was a city we all knew in different ways and to different extents, George best of all. A native of Larisa with the sturdy build if not the background of a Thessalian farm boy, he had studied there as an undergraduate in the late 1980s and still kept a cosy apartment for when he or his guests were in town. I think Thessaloniki was probably his favourite place, if not in the world at least in Greece. It had a modicum of culture and a sense of sophistication and style, most evident in its well-outfitted young women, sweetshops and well-lit bookstores, but was

less chaotic or congested than Athens. It was friend-
lier, though getting less so as the usual Western
commercialism seeped in, a commercialism which
the staunch anarchists and communists vaguely
affiliated with the Aristotle University downtown
tried to stave off with colourful protest banners and
a dedicated café presence, when they could afford
it, or through patronizing certain public benches
around which the mangy and formidable wild dogs
of Thessaloniki slept.

We had dinner at a swanky open-air eatery in
Kalamaria, the fashionable eastern suburb on the
water that at the time of the great fire of 1917 had
been a muddy village outside of the city. 'Do you like
the salad?' asked Neni.

'Not so much,' I replied. 'There's too much
lettuce and this ... dressing.' It was good I wasn't
very hungry. I had never liked lettuce but in Greece,
where there was a certain justice in tomatoes, onions,
cucumbers and peppers topped with feta cheese, olive
oil and oregano, it was more or less sacrilege. Seeing
any Greek enjoying a conventional Western salad

dismayed me; I regarded it with the kind of morbid dread a Byzantine patriarch would have reserved for the theological innovations of the Latin Church. It was a sign of creeping foreign contamination that threatened the sanctity of the whole – all the more menacing in that no one else seemed particularly bothered by lettuce.

Over the eight years that I had known Thessaloniki, the city had been becoming incrementally less Greek and more international, what with the British university degrees now for sale via affiliation courses, Starbucks coffee in the main square of Kamara and an embryonic Chinatown down from the gritty train station. And life had become much more expensive since the quiet euthanisation of the drachma in 2001. 'And it is getting worse,' murmured Neni, whose state employers had been several months late with everyone's salaries. Yet she still maintained her usual sunny disposition. Everyone complained about the euro, and I thought this was a reason to feel optimistic; complaining, at least, was a Greek trait of long-standing and immovable tradition.

Yet despite the changes there still were tangible reminders of Thessaloniki's past as the second city of the Byzantine Empire, a sort of Constantinople in miniature. They ran from the Byzantine walls that hemmed in the upper town's vivid old houses and the open markets of iced silvery fish to the venerable shops cluttered with nautical lanterns or ecclesiastical supplies or vats of pungent soup. When the rain lashed down in November, moving the café life indoors, men with the black beards and mournful eyes of Trebizond filled the windows playing backgammon. At night, the bouzoukis still warmed taverna guests with rembetika, that down-and-out music born of the Anatolian conflagration of 1922–3, when the Great Idea resolved into smoke and cinders and a million people crossed the sea, or didn't, in the refugee boats bound for Greece after the failed liberation of Smyrna.

The forced migrations which accompanied the end of the Ottoman Mediterranean shaped the character of the Greek province of Macedonia. It was a province which the Greeks had sought to 'liberate' for two decades, often led by the charismatic Eleftherios Venizelos, seven times prime minister during the first third of the 20th century. Venizelos achieved fame in his native Crete by challenging the steadily crumbling Ottoman rule of the island. In fact, Cretan troops loyal to him would play a key role in the *Makedonikos Agonas* ('Macedonian Struggle') of 1904–08, a turbulent and confusing multi-sided conflict heavy on propaganda and generally to the detriment of the local inhabitants, orchestrated by Serbia, Bulgaria, Greece and Ottoman Turkey, and complicated by a challenge from indigenous Macedonians, who fought for and against each other as the situation demanded. It was this Macedonia, not the ancient empire the world remembers today from schoolbook accounts of Alexander the Great, that would matter in the lakes region.

We had been driving very fast and the flat land of the ancient capital, where the tomb of Philip II of Macedon was discovered, had given way to green hills and sun as we approached Edessa late the following morning. It was the first authentic Macedonian town after the nondescript lowlands. The road up to it ribboned along the inside of a cliff and on the far side was an enormous waterfall, the most unusual feature apart from the glassed-in Alfa-Romeo dealership on the right.

We parked in the center, in front of a row of cafés. Stepping out of the car, I instantly felt the buoyancy of the air, filled with water from the falls. It had a cooling effect on what was becoming a hot day and leafy green trees attested to this lushness. I had been in Edessa, long ago, and had gone down into the thundering falls, in a dry crevice behind the rushing water, taking pictures of these huge sheets of water cascading down.

Edessa was the ancient name of the town that was resurrected in 1912, after Greek forces swept in during the Balkan Wars. It replaced the Slavic Macedonian name, Vodena, derived from the word *voda* (water), apparent testimony to the waterfall. Other villages and towns in Macedonia were renamed after Greece, allied with Serbia, Montenegro and Bulgaria, drove the Ottoman Turks almost completely out of Europe. It was the climax of the Macedonian Struggle and the newly 'liberated' province was neatly divided between the Balkan allies. Under Venizelos, the Greeks had doubled their territory practically overnight, reclaiming several Aegean islands and taking half of the geographical territory of Macedonia.

Bulgaria, however, also coveted the territory, looking nostalgically on the proto-Bulgar kingdom of the 10th century that had been centered in the lakes of Macedonia. Despite its large contribution of infantry and heavy casualties, Bulgaria had been granted only a tiny sliver of Macedonia, in the Pirin Mountains. The Bulgarians foolishly declared war on their erstwhile allies, were defeated, and lost the vital access to the Aegean they had won in Thrace. They also lost Adrianople to the Turks, who walked in without a fight. It was renamed Edirne.

Although large stretches of Macedonia did not have a majority Greek population in 1913, the doctrine of liberation rather than invasion was upheld at all costs. All of the levers of state power were used, especially the education system and the church, to strengthen Macedonia's Hellenic identity. After the destruction of the age-old Greek populations of Trebizond in the Pontus, ethereal Cappadocia and Smyrna and other Aegean cities in 1922, the Anatolian refugees were largely resettled in the new Greece of Macedonia and Thrace. Macedonia was now Greek, or at least half of it was, and Anatolian Greeks would become Macedonians.

The greatness of Alexander, the quintessential Macedonian, had been his ability to become Greek and to spread Greek ways far and wide, an achievement that brought Hellenism to North Africa and the Levant, to Anatolia and beyond. The Greeks had always excelled at assimilation. Many times it had saved them. But after 1913 they learned how to submit to self-assimilation without admitting, perhaps without even knowing, that it was being done to them. Much later, during the break-up of Yugoslavia in 1991, their descendents would argue that it was illogical for a foreign country to call itself Macedonia when there was an undeniably Greek province with the same name just to the south. There was nothing more Greek than the hard, straight blade of logic. The tutor of Alexander, by coincidence or historical asymmetry, was that great conqueror of logic, Aristotle. I remembered having seen, years earlier, a ruined podium in a Macedonian thicket where someone told us he had once lectured.

'Maybe we can eat something,' I said. I had not eaten anything at all and it was approaching midday. 'Okay,' said George. 'They must have some *pougatsa* places.' Pougatsa was always welcome. The flaky filo pie filled with golden cream and dusted with confectioner's sugar and cinnamon was, along with its close cousin *tyropita* (a crunchier filo pie stuffed with white cheese), a true Greek breakfast staple. The trick was to find it while it was still hot. We walked along the main street of handsomely-built Edessa with the wonderful freshness of water in the air and sure enough soon found a narrow bakery with a big glass window behind which the trays of tyropita and pougatsa lay. An energetic man in a black tee-shirt greeted us and we ordered three, to go. With rolling slices he chopped up the golden mass with the big curved-bladed baker's knife, artfully sprinkling the powdered sugar and cinnamon over them from their metal canisters and weighed them. The curved blade of the Greek bakery in the soft pie was always pleasurable to watch and it put things in perspective. Eating relaxed me and I stopped thinking of surreal histories and soon we considered coffee too.

We decided to defer that pleasure until the next town, Florina, known everywhere in Greece for its sweet red peppers. Soon we were in a new country of lush mountains occasionally broken by bare rugged hills with olive trees. It became overwhelmingly forested, and the road more winding. The sun had now completely replaced the grey skies over ancient Macedonia and it was turning out to be a very fine day indeed.

George had been making phone calls to find accommodation at the lakes. We had not known it, but this was the one weekend of the year when the Greek side of Prespa was heavily visited, due to the annual summer concerts sponsored by the Greek government. It was a relatively successful effort to bring visitors to this all-but-forgotten corner of the country, as far from the sea as you could get. Now almost everything was booked up.

Florina was a lovely town built against a narrow high mountain and George said it was one of the coldest places in Greece in the winter. In this respect and in some others, like the long line of cafés with their colourful awnings and strolling inhabitants, it was similar to the much larger town of Bitola, 14 kilometres to the north on the other side of the border. The frigid air of winter in Macedonia, the thinnest air I had ever encountered, hung indiscriminately over both.

'*Elliniko metrio*,' I replied to the waitress as we sat outside on soft café couches. The famed Greek coffee comes in three forms: without sugar (*sketo*), medium-sweet (*metrio*), or sweet (*gluko*) and is made in a small copper pot, often narrowing at the top, simmering with raw ground coffee until a leathery head forms and it can be poured. Elsewhere in the Balkans they called it Turkish coffee, and I remembered once mentioning this to a presumably neutral party, an animated Serbian waiter in Crete. 'No,' he had insisted. 'There is a big difference. The Greek coffee is always Javanese and better quality and more aromatic.' Then again, he had also attested that the Serbs would someday take Kosovo back from the Albanians. In Serbia they sometimes called it Serbian coffee. I forgot to ask whether that one was, according to his nomenclature, really Greek or Turkish.

'But there *is* something different about it,' I said. 'It's more bronze-coloured on the top, and a little sweeter.'

'What do they call it in … Skopje?' asked Neni. Greeks, even the nicest ones, rarely referred to their neighbours north of the border as Macedonians, relying on terms like 'Slavs' or 'Skopians' (after the Macedonian capital, Skopje) – something akin to describing all Englishmen as 'Anglo-Saxons' or 'Londoners'.

'Turkish,' I laughed. 'And in the rest of Macedonia too. When they want to be funny they call it Macedonian. But I think Turkish coffee really is a little different somehow from Greek coffee.'

'*Gallikos?*' said the waitress, bringing the glass

press and cup. Neni signalled for it. I did not know why the Greeks called simple filter coffee French. I just knew that I would never willingly drink it again, whatever you wanted to call it. Many foreigners like myself found Greco-Turkic coffee too acerbic and rough on the palate at first, but swore by it thereafter. For me, drinking filter coffee in Greece was a betrayal akin to lettuce in salad. I started feeling patriarchal again.

George, who was polished and well-travelled and Greco-Roman, had his usual espresso. Before Crete he had been painstakingly piecing together the lost papyri of ancient Greek philosophical texts that had been buried in ash for two millennia after a volcano erupted near the town of Herculaneum in southern Italy. He was part of a team at the research institute in Naples and he often spoke of how real Italian pizza was more delicate and light and without superfluous toppings. It was clearly a complicated world.

Florina had bursts of colour and stately shuttered old Macedonian houses and plenty of lounging young people, but Prespa awaited us. On the road the country became even more spectacular, empty of civilization, deep gorges and dense forests with tiny villages occasionally peeking out of the valley below. Signs warned of bears and at one point a flock of sheep, led heroically by a caramel-coloured dog with floppy ears, blocked our way. The air was very clear and my ears popped as we went up. This splendid forested sea was the real Macedonia, as different from the arid center and south of Greece as you could get, a land historically known for its hunters and trappers and quiet streams. 'This is so beautiful,' said Neni. 'I have never been here before. I am so glad I came.'

'Well, we are so glad to have you,' said George. 'And it is really something. Very beautiful indeed.'

We talked about many things as we approached Prespa, even of old England and the days when George and I met. 'What did you like best about Oxford?' asked Neni.

'I don't know,' I said. 'I remember night, and a dark lane beside an old college and you would see the contours of a gargoyle's head leering out of the fog. Or nine o'clock on a Sunday morning in the Bodleian

Library, when you are almost the only person there, and it is still and clean and the sunlight is coming through the window and the dust is in the air and you are holding a smooth old book. I liked that.'

'Interesting,' she said. 'And you?'

'Well, Oxford is really a remarkable place,' said George. 'I greatly enjoyed being in the presence of this large group of scholars who, even though they were studying many different things, still appreciated, and regarded highly the work of their peers ... this spirit of community, this I found really extraordinary.'

'It is interesting, how differently both of you remember the same place,' murmured the psychologist.

As we drove the signs told us we were getting close to Prespa. And then, after going up and up, we rounded a corner and started going down. And then the lake appeared, stretching out placidly in the sun. We pulled over at a place where the view was best.

'Marvellous,' said George, surveying the lake far below. 'So here we are.' Below the hill and before the lake was a long flat plain, and in the water a very small island. A far-off haze enveloped the mountains lurking on the other side, where Albania began. We still needed accommodation, but it was not too late and we could explore.

At the bottom of the hill the road forked parallel with the water and we crossed a land bridge dividing the Lesser and Greater Prespa Lakes. Soon we saw a sign. 'Well, shall we go to Psarades?' said George. 'It is meant to be a nice village.' We followed the winding road up a steep hill, where at a particularly tight corner was another vantage point for looking at the lake. On the battered guardrail at the side of the road someone had spray-painted MAKEDONIA = ELLAS ('Macedonia equals Greece') in big blue letters. The narrow strip of land dividing the Greater and Lesser Prespa Lakes lay to the right. The latter lies almost completely in Greek territory, except for a tiny south-western corner belonging to Albania. The former was divided between these two and the Republic of Macedonia, which possesses the majority of it.

We found Psarades at the end of a jutting headland

facing into the larger Prespa lake on both sides. In the center well-kept stone houses with red-tiled roofs stood, but further up behind they were more dilapidated. 'A lovely village,' pronounced George. An old man in a sea-captain's hat who had been sitting under a sort of wooden-railed pagoda with other village elders approached us.

George greeted him in Greek and we got to talking. The man offered us a boat trip in a caïque, the traditional small fishing boat of the lake people, for 20 euros. 'Maybe we should eat lunch instead,' said Neni. I agreed. They sat down at a table outside and ordered fish and Greek salad and I went to speak with the old men in the pagoda. '*Dobar den, kako ste?*'

They were pleasantly surprised to hear a foreigner bidding them good day in Macedonian. Outsiders rarely did. I had been right. After the inevitable explanations – I was an American, living in Skopje, writing – I asked if there was accommodation to be found. The sea-captain went to ask someone. 'Because of this concert weekend, everything is full,' he apologized.

'There is something interesting about these

people,' I said, back at the table. I pointed at the men in the pagoda under the robust Greek flag billowing in the sudden breeze. 'They were speaking to me in Macedonian. They said there are 80 people in this village and they are Macedonians.'

'Really!' said Neni. 'But they were speaking to us in Greek before.'

The Greek Civil War raged in the aftermath of World War II, with Communists and Nationalists battling for control. With the backing of the US and Britain, the Right won out. All were anxious lest the new Yugoslav government, which held the northern half of Macedonia, tried to fight for Greek-held Macedonia. Yet it was an irrational fear; Tito, a Croat Communist, was determined to suppress any ethnic nationalism in the new federation, whether it came from Serbs, Croats, Bosnians, Albanians or Macedonians. When Macedonian Communist Partisan fighters suggested taking the war to Aegean Macedonia (as they called the Greek side) they were taken out and shot as a warning to others.

In Greece itself, however, some Macedonians were

seduced by the Communists, who promised them an independent Macedonia after the Royalists had been defeated. In the bigger picture, the Macedonians of Greece became the first victims of the Cold War, as the Western powers sought to prevent Soviet-allied Bulgaria or Communist Yugoslavia from violating borders that had been established little over 30 years earlier. Greece had long been a favoured client state of Great Britain, due to the latter's own maritime interests. From 1946 to 1949, when the Communists were finally defeated, many thousands of Slavic Macedonians, Bulgarians and ethnically Greek Communists were expelled from Greek-held Macedonia. The Macedonian ones, many of them children, became known as the *begaltsi*, 'refugees', and were dispersed into the new Communist Yugoslavia or the Soviet Union. A law passed in 1982 decreed that only ethnically Greek refugees would be allowed to return.

'We didn't learn about this in school,' said Neni, looking around at the pretty stone houses. The wind whipped up and toppled an empty chair and in the

22

soft grass far below by the lake bulls were stubbornly locking horns. George was not particularly nationalistic but he disliked history, I felt, in the same way James Joyce had. 'People who live in border areas always speak the other language,' he said. It was better not to let the fish get cold.

The Prespa speciality, carp, was savoury and golden and carved up into fillets. It was delicious with lemon and we washed it down with beer. The portions were huge, plates piled with fish and a hefty salad with plenty of oil for dipping the country bread in. It was a very satisfying lunch and too much to finish. Compared to the prices in Thessaloniki, it was also scandalously cheap.

After lunch we explored Psarades, crowded with narrow stone stairways and alleys wrapping up around tight clustered stone houses. From somewhere inside of them was conveyed the Macedonian language; old rugs hung from their blue-painted wood balconies and the clothes of old people dried in the soft breeze. In many places the white plaster was chipped away. But despite that some old houses were crumbling and unoccupied, the village seemed to be holding together well enough.

In Greek, the name Psarades means 'fishermen' – the principal livelihood of the inhabitants, at least those young enough to work. At 81, Kuzman was probably in retirement. I found him sitting on a stone ledge with his wife, Theodora. He had a baseball cap and a wooden walking stick and the slouch of someone used to leaning forward to catch what was being said. The old woman wore a shawl and slippers and a dress with small flowers on it and she stared beatifically into the evening, hands folded on her lap.

Occasionally a Macedonian diaspora group from Canada or Australia would come to check on such people and lament the Greek government's non-recognition of its Macedonian minority. But life was good enough, they said. Before the Greek Civil War, the village – they called it Nivici, a Macedonian word for a certain kind of small Prespa fish – had around 1,100 inhabitants and 300 children in the school. 'Now there are almost no young people left,' said Kuzman.

The couple had met during the Civil War. Fate had cast them on different sides; she fought for the Communists, he for the Nationalists. There was another old man sitting on a bench and George and Neni were talking to him. When the Communists came, they conscripted him, though he did not embrace the cause. He was not deported with other Macedonians because the villagers vouched for him before a military tribunal.

Dusk was approaching and we bade farewell to the old people of Psarades, heading down and over the land-bridge between the two lakes to the village of Plati, where George had somehow arranged lodgings. The new 'pensione' of the village was a grandiose, two-storey modern structure with a lawn and small pool. A balding middle-aged man who bore an uncanny resemblance to the Kosovo Albanian prime minister and alleged war criminal, Agim Ceku, greeted us emphatically and smiled.

'It *is* kind of mafia,' George conceded, going up the stair. 'But what can we do? Everything in the whole area is booked.'

He had a point. The locals had to make the most of their one weekend a year of real business and the price was easily double what it should have been. But no matter. It was a large enough room with kitchen facilities and an extra bedroom, just fine for our needs. 'Now let's take a rest and get ready for the concert.'

After an hour we were off to the nearby island of Saint Achilles (Agios Achilleos), where the concert was to be held. The others were very excited about the evening, which promised to be revelatory, as it would feature the great national singer, George Dalaras, performing a great national epic poem, the *Axion Esti* of Odysseas Elytis. It had been put to music by the composer Nikos Theodorakis, known to foreigners for *Zorba the Greek*.

They did not let us to drive all the way. All concert-goers were signalled to park in a dusty field with trampled dead grass reminiscent of an Indiana state fair. There were whistling, waving policemen, who put groups of 50 of us onto buses which drove us to where a very long wooden bridge was floating on Lesser Prespa Lake. Periodic lights guided the way, revealing huge bunches of reeds and black water. There were more energetic guards, the smell of pork *souvlaki* cooking and Greek music in the air. All in all, it was a fearsome display of organized Hellenism.

Agios Achilleos was once a great center of Byzantine civilization, and the capital of the 10th-century Slavic ruler Tsar Samuel, whose territory briefly incorporated parts of Greece, Bulgaria, Macedonia and Serbia. Yet now it had only a handful of inhabitants. Ruined old houses, maybe from Ottoman times, certainly older than the Greek Civil War, lay about near the ones that had been restored.

We reached the semi-circular ruins of Samuel's grand basilica, where the stage and instruments had been set up, and we climbed up the hill before it and staked out a place among the packed crowd. Many people were holding small white candles and the vast sky was full of stars. In musical performances as in religion, the Greeks always respected the aesthetics of natural settings. 'This is something unusual, a very rare treat,' said George. 'I have never heard the whole poem performed at once.'

'Tell me,' I said, 'what makes it so special?'

'Well, the *Axion Esti* is a beloved thing for us. The title means "It Is Worthy",' said George. 'It is about life and love and death. Presumably, life is worth living – this is the essential point. The poem's structure was inspired by Byzantine hymnography, Elytis said, and it is very interwoven with Greek identity. So it is a very high intellectual achievement which has won popular appreciation – people actually sing it.'

'Really!' I said. 'I can't imagine people singing a poem today.'

'Well, Theodorakis did a very good job,' said George. 'He worked for a long time on it, because he wanted to do it justice. He said that the adaptation would have to inspire the same feelings as the poem. The poem was also inspired by the bad memories of the Greek Civil War. But the real achievement of Theodorakis was that he made a poem into public property.'

As the opening acts and speeches from enterprising politicians went on, more people kept streaming in. Perhaps there were 5,000. Obviously many other Greeks agreed with George that it would be a special event.

'So who is this Dalaras, anyway?' I asked.

'Well, Dalaras is quite a character,' said George. 'And a very controversial one. He has been accused of embracing the cause of Cyprus purely for profit, and of jumping on the backs of younger artists, to advance his own career.'

'He is old, but he does have a rich voice,' added Neni. 'He had a feud with another singer, Tzimis Panousis, who attacked Dalaras about his support for Cyprus. Dalaras sued him, and Panousis was not allowed to say Dalaras out loud –'

'So instead he started referring to Dalaras as *Akatonomos*,' said George.

'It means The Unspeakable – but we also use it to mean the devil,' concluded Neni.

Dalaras was a real Greek. There was no doubt about him. After a few minutes more he was brought out and introduced to the crowd: Dalaras, the *Laikos Tragoudistis* – Folk Singer, or Singer of the People

– and everyone clapped and cheered and Dalaras acknowledged them and the performance began.

The *Axion Esti* started like a swirl of seabirds calling, with irregular drums and echoes from behind, a chime, then brief silence. And there was Dalaras, like an opera singer, sonorous and preposterous all at the same time. The music became a moving thing, friendly, warm, a wave of voices, a sea.

The movement continued with drums and hints of the east, the Asia Minor that was lost, and later an unnerving 'dant-dant-da-da-dant' and a chorus of respondents gradually reaching a crescendo. But it went on for a very long time and with many movements and Dalaras began calling off the Greek islands by name and the children in front of us became restless.

The crowd was livened up, however, by the parts that were less abstract and which everyone knew and they began to chant along with Dalaras the Unspeakable and things reached a triumphant finale. Then it was time to tramp down the hill to where the delectable smell of roasting meat was coming from.

'So, what did you think?' said Neni.

'It was very good,' I said. 'Not like what I expected, though.'

'How so?' asked George.

'Well, to be honest, I didn't know what to expect from a poem being put to music. Maybe I thought it would be more ... Homeric, rarified. But it was like taverna music in some parts. Actually, some parts sounded like a commercial for pasta sauce.'

'For pasta sauce!' laughed Neni. '*Ela, re!*'

'What did it mean, the line that everyone was singing along with?' I asked. 'I couldn't make it out.'

'It means "sun of justice, don't forget my country," said George. 'Elitis was referring to the desperation and suffering of the Greek Civil War.'

We reached the place where the bridge was and the crowd was still boisterous. A long grill had been set up and we queued up for the sticks of souvlaki. There was not the usual pita bread but hunks of rough bread instead. 'How many do you want?' said George. 'I will have three.'

We sat on a ledge and watched the people filing

out on the floating bridge and ate. 'We should definitely come back here and see this island in daylight,' said George between mouthfuls.

Gradually the masses dwindled but it was still crowded before the bridge. There was a deep lake smell on the cool air and the moon shone down from clear skies. In the moonlight and in the artificial light that had been prepared for the special event you could see the ruins of the houses abandoned long ago. The visitors were satisfied with the concert and with Dalaras. As they crossed the bridge they were still singing the epic line: *Sun of justice, don't forget my country.*

Chapter 2

In the morning I was awoken by sunshine coming through the embroidered drapes and I went outside to have coffee while my companions slept. It was a beautiful day and the man who had resembled the war criminal the day before, Stratos, was not at all bad. He had been to America and spoke highly of Boston, as well as other cities I hardly knew. We spoke in English and Greek and Macedonian and I asked for Turkish coffee. His father was also sitting there with some other old-timers in front of the pool and the outdoor bar where they prepared the coffee.

His father was 81 years old and spoke in halting tones but fast enough and mostly in Greek. During the war, the old man had been arrested by Tito's Partisans, in Kavadarci, in the heart of the Macedonian republic's arid wine country, and tried to escape to Greece; 'but there the Greek fascists imprisoned him too,' concluded Stratos. 'I spent two-and-a-half months with the Communists here,' said the old man, 'but I saw they were just lying and I left.'

'How long has your family been in this area?' I asked.

'More than 500 years ago, some of our ancestors came from Mariovo,' said Stratos. 'They were four or six families – the Ottomans wanted workers for a village on the lake.'

Mariovo is an unsettling place, a plain with deep gorges and rivers and rock formations that hum with an unearthly energy, in a triangular area in the south of the Macedonian republic, between Bitola and Gevgelija and the Greek mountain border. Once a thriving community of villages, it was devastated during the wars. Today this vast area is sparsely inhabited, though the ghost villages remain and the government has hinted at turning them into weekend cottages for foreign emissaries in Skopje.

'A hundred years ago, in the time of Ilinden, did

the people here consider themselves Macedonians, or Greeks, or Bulgarians?' I asked. I wasn't asking the old man; I was asking him to ask the memories of his father and grandfather and whoever came before that. Ilinden was an uprising organized against the Turks in the summer of 1903 for Macedonian independence, or perhaps for greater Bulgaria; it led, for all of two weeks, to the first republic in the Balkans, at the mountain stronghold of Krusevo west of Prilep. Macedonians and Bulgarians alike claim it as their heritage. The ephemeral president, Nikola Karev, promised beautiful ideals of equality and brotherhood for all in the new state. The Turks put down the revolt with great bloodshed, committing numerous atrocities in the villages.

For the old man, the story went back to 1878, and the short-lived Treaty of San Stefano following the Russo-Turkish war. Tsarist forces liberated Bulgaria from the Ottomans and marched to within a few miles of Constantinople itself, causing great alarm in Britain, France and the Austro-Hungarian Empire. The Treaty of San Stefano awarded Bulgaria most of

Macedonia, but this was intolerable for the European Great Powers, as it represented the encroachment of Russian influence in the Balkans and Aegean. Another conference was thus set up, this time in Berlin, which restricted Bulgaria's gains tremendously – an affront which was never forgotten and which soon led to the creation of secret societies, terrorist groups, outlaw bands and political fronts throughout the Balkans.

'At first, they fought for the freedom of Macedonia,' said the old man, 'but then the Bulgarians took over. They sent people from Bulgaria to organize their propaganda. So did the Greeks. In the end, they fought for Greece or Bulgaria, not for Macedonia.'

'What about the language?' I said. 'Did they call it Macedonian?'

Yes,' he said. 'The people here spoke Macedonian, but were told they were Greeks. My grandfather couldn't speak any Greek, but he sided with them anyway. Then there were the Exarchists, who called themselves Bulgarians and supported the Bulgarian Orthodox Church's position here. Then there were the Centralists and the Vrhovists,' added the old man.

'And Pavlos Melas organized Greeks here to fight the Turks and the Bulgars.'

'Very complicated.'

'However,' he said, 'all of our history is ultimately Byzantine.'

George and Neni woke up sometime late in the morning and I found the bathroom floor was perfectly mopped. 'He is a good army boy,' said Neni. 'He's always doing that. He was doing that when we were in Chios this summer.'

We ate something and had another coffee with the men downstairs, who offered some information about the water birds to be found on the lake. 'Shall we go back to Agios Achilleos?' said George. It seemed like a fine idea and so we said farewell to our hosts and crossed the little land-bridge between the Lesser and Greater Prespa Lakes, as orange-billed pelicans flapped past overhead.

The lake and the island looked completely different in daylight. The floating bridge also looked less infinite, now that we could see the other side and there were no crowds. The water's surface was rippled and reflected the huge billowing clouds and reeds that rustled in the breeze. The lake was set perfectly, as if by Providence, against tawny mountains touching clouds that looked like snow. A small barge was ferrying army trucks back to the mainland from the island, where they had apparently been kept during the concert in case of emergency.

We reached the basilica, where the concert had been held. It was now a different place, empty of people but filled with light and songbirds and ancient stone. In the darkness it had been impossible to realize what a magnificent structure it must have been. Only half of the wall on the left survived, curving out into a rounded apse in the center, all set against a mountain on the Greek side of the lake. An enormous courtyard of flat stones survived leading up to the basilica ruins where large sections of medieval brick walls and sculpted pillars stood exposed to the open air, central beams jutting out of the white mortar and hewn logs too. We traipsed all over the open structure in search of photo opportunities.

'Eek!' said Neni. 'There are too many lizards!'

'And too little time,' I said.

We left the ruins, passing up the hill where we had sat for the music the night before. A stray bull was chewing grass and from the top the view of the basilica against the mountains was even more spectacular. We kept walking in the open land, through olive trees and grass and thistle, and the higher we got the further you could see and the more sublime the lake appeared, stretched against the mountains and the clouds and the more I could appreciate the Byzantine builders' church location. A cluster of ashes and olives lay in a circle where someone had lit a fire and we reached another church, this one complete and white and of much more recent design.

'I think there is supposed to be another very old church ruin somewhere,' said George. 'Shall we find it?'

We went back where we had come, and where the island's little bit of life – a shop, a restaurant – was. An old woman sitting in the shade by a ramshackle house with chickens out front told us to go up the road in the other direction. We trudged along and the houses, some of which had clearly once been grand structures, became increasingly desolate and destroyed. Even the nature felt it, with broken scrub trees and stinging nettles and smooth jagged logs like driftwood scattered along the ground. Perhaps the weather on this side of the island was harsher? Beyond the western side of the lake, on the forested shore, was the final territory of Greece; beyond that lay Albania.

We went on for too long and realized that the church had eluded us. Returning, we found that sure enough very little remained of it – little more than a depression in the earth with some stones that George nevertheless clambered down to inspect. It was very small, compared to the basilica, but still would have been well placed with its contemplative position overlooking the quiet western waters.

Back down at the entrance to the island, at the bridge, bulls idly ate alongside caïques in the rich grass. To the left a wild castaway's house of weathered boards strung with fishing nets – probably ornamental, but you never know – floated against the reeds and to the right diminutive lily pads shimmered and dragonflies darted over them and the black brackish water on which they lay. A cow bellowed. 'I reckon that people don't swim in this lake much,' I said.

'No, I would think not,' said George.

'But they do in the big Prespa lake, at least on the Macedonia side,' I said.

'Really!'

'Yes, it is much cleaner – and deeper,' I said. We were crossing the bridge now and heading back. I had always had a fear of lakes. I had grown up on a dank pond in central Massachusetts infested with 10-foot weeds that would allegedly wrap around your ankles and drag you down, as well as snapping turtles that would finish you off. Then there were the mosquitoes.

'What is a snapping turtle?' said Neni.

'It is a ferocious and cranky turtle with a sharp curved beak. It likes to bite people, hence its name.'

'I am afraid of turtles,' admitted Neni.

'What is the word in Greek for "turtle?" I forgot,' I asked.

'*Helonas*,' said George.

'So we have a new word for this special case – Helonophobia, fear of turtles.'

'Ah yes, so I have Helonophobia,' said Neni. 'Look at them!'

Up ahead bearing down on us on the bridge was a black-clad Orthodox priest walking briskly with an army of old women similarly dressed behind him. He was carrying a large cardboard box of presumably priestly implements and the women each carried small Chinese take-away paper boxes containing an unknown substance.

'Are they widows?' I asked.

'Maybe yes, maybe no,' said George warily. 'We should take care. There must be some religious ceremony today at the church.' The peculiar line of parishioners snaked all the way back to the bridge so that by the time we had reached it they were still getting on. 'It must be a big ceremony,' I said.

There was another village to see along the way, Agios Germanos, and it would make a fine stop for lunch. I had been there once, a long time before, on a weekend trip during a language course in Thessaloniki. In Prespa they had put me with an old Irishman who had retired and devoted the rest of his life to learning foreign languages. He was not a quick learner but he was very kind. I remembered the frescoes on the rock below Psarades, which can only be reached by boat. George had suggested seeing them again but there was no time. We had to eat lunch and run Neni back to Florina in time to catch the last bus to Thessaloniki, as it was Sunday and she had to work in the morning.

Agios Germanos was lovely and well kept, snug in the embrace of bare hills. Its old stone houses had been restored and it had a very old Byzantine church. It was a warm afternoon and we sat outside in the garden of a taverna, almost the only guests, and endeavoured to order everything.

The best way to eat, as always, was by ordering many plates of appetizers – what the Greeks call *mezedes* – which included local specialties. In addition to succulent ribs and another bulky Greek salad, there were *tsuknidopita*, crunchy filo pies filled with nettles (purportedly not of the stinging variety), as well as gobs of *ksinotiri*, sour cheese flecked with oregano and doused in olive oil, sweet Macedonian red peppers and more Prespa fish. Light beer was ideal for the thirst brought on by mild sunburn and exertion and time was forgotten about due to the good conversation and sound of rushing water from a creek down below. The harmony was complemented when a white cat and a white dog sat by my feet, mournfully and successfully begging for their lunch.

It was a very good lunch and everyone said so. 'Replenishment,' added George.

'It was almost poetic, the way that the oil clung to the cheese,' I said.

'Poetic?' questioned Neni.

'Don't forget, poetry is like a pasta sauce commercial.'

'Ha ha ha.'

The church of Agios Germanos, built in the early 11th century, was very close to the taverna. The rounded terracotta domes and striated brickwork marked it out as Byzantine and inside, where it was very dark and very narrow, could be seen the faded frescoes under restoration. 'Maybe it was built under the command of Patriarch Germanos in Constantinople, or by a monk of that name. But it may be the case that the patriarch was exiled,' said George.

'Hmm,' said Neni.

'This was really the hinterland of the empire,' he continued. 'It was as far away from Constantinople as you could get. Prespa was thus considered a place of exile at various times.'

We made it back to Florina while there was still plenty of light and pulled into the small bus station where the big buses waited rumbling. I said goodbye to Neni and then George did and we were suddenly alone. Coping with this new and startling situation required a stop for another coffee on Florina's elegant and colourful little street of cafés.

George had bought a newspaper and was reading it. George Bush was doing something on the front page.

'Don't forget, the terrorists hate us for our freedom,' I drawled.

'No. Women hate us for our freedom.'

'Ha!'

'So, boy, we got to Albania,' laughed George. 'Marvellous.' He was a good sport. He had wanted to stay another night in Greece. But I had been given the phone number of a Macedonian man who was a sort of local leader in one Macedonian-inhabited village on the Albanian side of the lake. By text message he had informed me that his village, Pustec, was only 25 kilometres from the border and that a man would be waiting for us at the hotel – a done deal.

'See, it will be easy,' I said. 'I hope so,' said George. 'But remember this is Albania we're talking about. Anything can happen.'

'You know what I read once?' I said brightly. 'That they have roads that just end.'

'That just … end?'

'Yeah! Isn't that funny?' I said. 'Maybe they got tired of building them, or ran out of money, I don't remember why. Same thing with the street lights.'

I could tell this was not making the driver and new owner of a very nice Volkswagen particularly enthusiastic and so I decided to accentuate the positive instead. 'But we *do* have this local contact who has arranged everything for us, and the people are all Macedonian there, so we won't have problems with the language,' I said. 'It will be fine.'

With that we left, back down the winding road through the mountains towards Prespa where we had to look out for the southern road to the Albanian border. The conversation turned to the tortured subject of politics somewhere near Pisoderi. I was on again about the Macedonians who had been driven out of Greece and how almost every village and town in Greek Macedonia had a forgotten name and secret, unspeakable history, or maybe two or three.

'I will not argue with that, since I don't really know,' said George. 'But what Greeks don't understand is why the people from Skopje cannot compromise and agree to a different name for their country.'

'How can they compromise on what they consider themselves to be?' I said.

'Well, it's just that for Greeks, Macedonia is a very sensitive issue. They feel that the people from Skopje

47

are trying to steal our history. I mean, do they really think they are descendents of Alexander the Great?'

'I think the standard view is that the Slavic tribes that arrived originally must have intermingled with whoever was left of the ancient Macedonians. But I think they would see Alexander more in affectionate terms, like an old grandfather or something.'

'But,' continued George, 'the name does imply something, both historical and some territorial claims … If they take this name which does not really belong to them – *this* Greeks object to.'

'I can assure you the tanks are not about to roll into Greece,' I said. 'They are not interested in territory. What solution do you suggest?'

'I don't know,' said George. 'I think "Slavo-Macedonia" was suggested as a compromise.'

'Well, that is viewed as a slur,' I explained. 'Plus, the Albanian minority would get crazy and argue that they were not included in the name.'

'Also Skopje could be "Upper Macedonia",' considered George.

'In the sense of geographical realities, that would

48

be fair,' I said. 'But then would Greece start to call Greek Macedonia "Lower Macedonia"?'

He looked perplexed. 'No, of course not.'

'Well, that's not very fair, is it?' I said. 'It's like with feta cheese and the Greek court case in the EU where they won the exclusive rights to that brand name. Greece wants the "Macedonia" brand exclusively.'

He did not want to agree but I had a point. 'What do the people there think of Greeks?' he said.

'They like Greeks very much. They are only sad about the politics.'

We stopped in Pisoderi for a few minutes. It was a tiny village, a collection of steep square houses nestled in forests. The dying light of evening reflected on the houses, accentuating the geometry of it. People were sitting out on a balcony opposite and behind the building that announced itself as a hotel there was a small overgrown cemetery, and below it where the mountain began deep enchanting forests of densely packed pines. It reminded me somehow of Ireland; you could enter those woods, I imagined, and never return, pulled into the other world, becoming a prisoner of a Macedonia that was unseen and perhaps never existed. Maybe I already was. I turned around quickly.

It was time to go. We reached the road where it forked left to the south and less than a mile before the border we stopped at the last petrol station in Greece. 'We had better fill up here,' said George. 'Who knows if we will find something on the other side.'

He was a little nervous and darkness was approaching but we forged ahead. At the Greek border the only car in front of us was a big black American SUV with Albanian license plates. A man in a black suit was standing at the window and laughing with the policeman inside. Waiting for him was an alluring, scantily-dressed Albanian girl who said she was a journalist from Korce, a town not far from the border. Like many people in Albania, she spoke some Italian, which our resident Renaissance man was very happy to utilize.

'Well ... bye,' she smiled, as her sponsor came back with their passports and opened the car with black windows.

'Did you see that guy?' I said. 'So mafia.'

'What a shame,' pronounced George. 'Maybe if the situation had been different …'

The other side of the border was somewhat less stimulating. A guard in a pitifully threadbare uniform was stationed in a small and dimly-lit hut. 'Ten euro, 10 euro, visa,' he said.

'Even for Greeks?' asked George. 'For Americans?' I added.

'Everybody, everybody, 10 euros for visa.'

'Just to come here for two days,' I said to George, shaking my head. 'Amazing.'

After the border the world dissolved into darkness. 'So,' said George. 'This is Albania. Boy! We are here.'

The road was flat and straight and the sense of being on another planet grew very strong. There were no lights, and the only occasional signs for villages led to sparse and small evilly-lit settlements.

'This nothingness … it's almost existential,' I remarked.

There were still no signs for Pustec, or Liqenas as

51

it was called in Albanian, and we had been driving for longer than I had expected. The headlights occasionally exposed marvellous sights such as men sitting in the dark on the side of the road in plastic chairs, apparently watching the cars for amusement.

'Did you see them, just sitting there? What the hell is this place?'

'I have never seen anything like this,' said George. I began to think he was considering the value of his car insurance policy.

'Let's stop at the next gas station and ask someone where to go. It must have been on the right but back there somewhere, the lake is on that side.'

'Okay.'

Eventually we pulled in at a lit petrol station where two policemen were operating a speed trap with the help of what looked to be a 19th-century camera on a rickety tripod, except that it had no black cloth for sticking your head under. The policemen were friendly and communicative, though they couldn't understand anything we said. A very great thing about George was his propensity to speak in full, rational, well-articulated English sentences to people who could not understand a word he was saying. 'Excuse me, we are looking for the road to Pustec. Do you know where that is?'

I simplified. 'Pustec, Pustec – Liqenas?'

One of the policemen's eyes lit up. With some form of sign language we were told to turn around and take the third left to the village of Gorica, which cheered me somewhat, considering this was a Macedonian name and as such had to be near Pustec. We thanked the officers and left them to their strange contraption.

Finally we saw a small turn-off to the left where an old man was standing in front of a building. 'Gorica?' I yelled. He pointed us down the turn-off and onto a crumbling road. 'Well,' said George, 'I guess this is it.'

It did not look promising. It was pitch black, but the promise of 26 kilometres made it seem possible. Gradually, however, the road began rising and we were going up a mountain, though we could not see anything except the immediate sides of the road which disintegrated in parts, helpfully over raw cliff edges. At a branch in the road we tried the left and got even more nowhere than the nowhere we had already found. We resolved to just keep going up. The road zigzagged and there was no one, or almost no one on it, save for a pick-up truck or two that barrelled by with small militias of young toughs in the back.

'We could ask someone if we are on the right road,' said George.

'And they could just rob and kill us,' I mused. 'A car with Greek license plates, in the middle of nowhere ... who would ever know?'

It was an unsettling thought. The only thing was to keep on driving. I was beginning to feel very guilty that I had forced George to drive on that night when he was clearly tired and when we had no map or idea where we were going. I sent a message to my wife in Skopje to call our mysterious contact and see what was going on. The reply came.

'Well, looks like we won't be seeing our man,' I said. 'He is stuck in Bitola or Resen and he won't get there till tomorrow.'

George frowned slightly but kept calm. He was always calm in serious situations, which was in itself calming. 'So, what do we do? Should we continue on, or go back and maybe try to find Korce?'

'Well, he told her to tell us that we should still go to the hotel in Pustec and ask for Kiko Ago.'

'Who?'

'Well, the manager of the hotel.'

'And he is a Macedonian?'

'I guess so.'

'Did you tell your wife that we are basically lost?' George asked.

'Well, sort of ... let's just continue a while and if we don't find anything soon, we will turn back. Are you okay to drive?'

'Yes, I am fine,' said George, who was watching very intently to ensure that we did not drive over a cliff. He laughed. 'Remember, I moved up from Team Renault to Team Volkswagen! I'm ready for a challenge.'

I winced. It was a very nice car and I did not want to be responsible for its destruction.

It was now nearly eleven o'clock and we were still no closer to anywhere though it did seem we had reached a ridgeline and the road was evening out. This at least was good. The winding road had disintegrated several times from crumbling asphalt to dirt but now it was becoming more stable. On the other hand, if we did not find something soon, we would have to go back down to where we came and then be back on the black highway of existential disorientation which supposedly led to Korce. Either way, things were not auspicious.

Then something happened which was very great, the first certifiably great thing of the night. 'Hey!' I exclaimed. 'A normal road – this must go somewhere!'

Indeed, we had come out onto a newly asphalted stretch of road and not a moment too soon. George was heroic and impassive but it was hard to square being lost for over an hour at night in the middle of Albania, especially if you were a philosopher and especially if you were in your own vehicle.

'This is a good sign,' he agreed.

'Ha!' I said. 'And I was just starting to think maybe we were on one of those roads that just end, remember that?'

He did and we were glad we were not on such a road.

Until it ended.

'What's this?' said George, slamming to a halt. The silky asphalt tarmac with the solid mountain on the left and black nothingness on the right had run out and in its place was an obscure and rocky goat track. 'Should we go in there?'

'Roads that just end,' I repeated, as if in a trance. 'Uh, I don't think so. Let's go back to where the road forked, remember we took the top one instead of the one going down? Maybe we should have done that.'

'All right,' he said, pulling off an 18-point-turn in the hollow of the mountain. 'Roads that just end. This Albania is really something.'

We reached the point where the roads split and took the one leading down. 'Well at least this is a good asphalt road too,' I said. 'It's got to be leading to Pustec.'

We drove on in the blackness and after a while an unsettling feeling overcame us. It was confirmed when the asphalt ended at a rocky trail that was very similar or the same to the one we had just been stopped at.

'What the fuck,' I yelled. 'This is like something out of the *Twilight Zone*.'

'Maybe ... maybe we should think about just going to Korce and find this village in the morning,' said George.

'Okay, okay,' I said. I was very angry at having come so far and being so completely lost. I read the text message again: *twenty-six kilometres. You'll be there in thirty minutes*. Clearly, the road to Pustec was paved with good intentions.

Then the phone rang. It was my wife. 'Did you make it yet?'

'No, and we are going to have to go to Korce,' I said wearily. 'What a disaster.'

'But you are safe? You are okay?'

'Yes, yes, just very pissed off.'

Then suddenly something happened that could

only have occurred in a dream or as a sign of fate. Out of the total blackness to our left emerged a ghostly figure: in the middle of nowhere, an old man wearing some sort of a poncho riding side-saddle on a burro laden down with sticks. I informed my wife.

'Well ask him! Maybe he knows where Pustec is!'

'Okay!'

I shouted out the window at the enigmatic figure: 'Pustec, Pustec, *kade e?*' ('where is it'?)

As if on cue the old man extended his hand providentially down a long and rock-strewn dirt track. 'This is the way to Pustec,' he responded in Macedonian. 'I am going there too.'

'Hey, we did it!' I shouted.

'Great,' said my wife. 'Send me a message if you get there!'

George took a deep breath and pointed the new Volkswagen down the steep and rocky path. 'You realize if we do this we cannot turn around,' he said.

'It's your car,' I said, 'Either way is fine with me.'

'Okay. We will try.'

The man on the donkey was somewhere behind

us, though we were moving infinitely more slowly than he. 'Unfuckingbelievable,' I said, shaking my head. 'What are the odds? Pancho Villa on a donkey, at eleven o'clock at night, on a mountain in the middle of nowhere in Albania? You could *not* make this stuff up!'

'It is really quite extraordinary,' admitted George.

We drove down the pitted path, each crunch of the undercarriage seeming more painful since we did not know when it would stop; however, the trip lasted only 15 minutes or so and we smoothed out onto old asphalt and there were a cluster of old cottages leading up to a well-lit area. A group of teenage girls was standing on one side of the street.

'Stop,' I said.

They were surprised to see strangers and very polite and very Macedonian. We had done it. We were in Pustec, a tiny Macedonian enclave on the other side of Lake Prespa from where we began, and now we just needed the hotel.

'It is after the center of the village, ask someone

60

again there,' said one of the girls. We drove on past old thatched houses of wood or stone like in any Macedonian village to what appeared to be a central point.

'Should we ask these boys?'

Two of them were on foot and their friends were in cars. They told us to follow them and the hotel would not be far, but it was down on the lake.

'Should we follow them?' said George. I thought he was slightly nervous with no one speaking English or Greek or Italian or French or Spanish or even German.

'We don't have much choice,' I said.

We went down past the houses which suddenly looked like better options, very cozy and inviting rather than broken-down and desolate and again it was dark though at least we could see lights far below. 'That must be the lake,' said George. 'Good.'

Finally we arrived at a small hotel on the black lake under trees. There were at least 20 cars in front. Some were old, but some were new. 'A Mercedes in Pustec?' said George. 'This I can't believe.'

The sound of loud, live Macedonian folk music

and many people could only mean one thing: a wedding. '*Da, imame svadba sega*'– 'Yes, we are having a wedding now,' said a teenage boy standing with his friends on the steps of the hotel.

Inside was a large open space with around 70 people of all ages, including the classic village great-grandmothers in shawls and old dresses and there was a band with an enormous synthesizer and a guitarist and other instrumentalists, and the guests were partaking in that great communal dance of three steps, the *oro*. I remembered it well from my own wedding. It had been infernally difficult but George, who was the godfather of the event, had done it effortlessly and the band then played *Zorba the Greek* in his honour and soon my wife's uncles took a great liking to him, arm-in-arm at shoulder level. There was also a gypsy brass band, but that was a different animal. There was no gypsy brass band in Pustec, probably because it was too damn hard to find, I thought. But there was a hotel and it was ours and now it would be a simple matter of checking in.

Or not.

'But we were told to come here by Edmond, from your village, and to find Kiko Aga as you see' – I displayed the lit phone text – 'from this message.'

'Yes, but he is not here now.'

'Can you check us in anyway?'

'No, there is no manager here now,' the boy said.

'What does he say?' asked George.

'He says there is no manager here. Imagine that. There is a full-blown wedding going on and they say no one is in charge.'

If we waited for an unspecified length of time someone might come to help us, they said. It was all too bizarre. But the boy really was trying. He led me to the lakefront, under wispy trees, where suddenly my phone switched from the Albanian to the Macedonian mobile operator signal; 'It reaches just this far,' he said. 'We come here to call Macedonia.' I called home and my wife had some words with the boy. 'He is trying to help you,' she said. 'Be patient, they will find you a room. How is George?'

'I think he is tired of this,' I said. 'But at least we made it.'

63

A few minutes later, in front of the hotel, the music was still pulsating and a beautiful girl in a revealing dress was standing in front of us and talking with the boy. 'What does she say?' said George. 'Well,' I said, 'it sounds like she wants to give us her room!'

'Really!' exclaimed George. 'But what about her?'

'Um ... Well, I don't *think* that she comes with it.'

They led us up a narrow outdoor flight of stairs which had no handrail and through a door to a narrow hallway with rooms on either side. They opened the second and we went in. The girl was working for the hotel, which appeared to double as a family home and which did not see many guests. There were two beds. 'I'm sorry, but we don't have any sheets,' the boy apologized. 'It is fine,' I said, 'we will manage. Thank you so much.'

We had done it. George sank into the bed and exhaled. 'Boy! We made it!'

'Would you like to go out?' I asked.

'Go out! Where?'

'The people here tell me there is a *zabava* tonight up in Pustec.'

What is a zabava?'

'A party,' I said.

'A party? In Pustec? Well, this we will have to see!'

The water did not work very well but we managed to wash up a little. 'At least the car's still there,' George noted. In the village we parked in front of a new-looking building out of which very loud Serbian pop music and young people were spilling onto the street.

'This must be ... the zabava?' said George.

Inside was a long wide room and down the center of it ran a lacquered double-sided wooden bench like in a German beer hall. On the sides of the room, which looked bigger than it was due to the general lack of furnishings, were small tables. On one side of the room were the boys, on the other side the girls. A disco ball presided over both and straight ahead was a small aperture where I presumed the drinks to be waiting. They all stared at us as we came in.

'This is incredible,' I whispered. 'Unreal.'

At the counter a middle-aged woman and young man were working. We ordered beer; it was Skopsko, imported from Macedonia and we could pay in Macedonian denars. Pustec was truly a lost piece of Macedonia, stranded on the other side of an arbitrary border.

We sat at a small table in the near corner and the people looked at us with curiosity for a while and then went back to their own conversations. They were teenagers and were dressed up, especially the girls, as if they were out for a night in a posh city club rather than in a forgotten village on a forgotten lake under a mountain in Albania.

I was very happy. 'You see, George, they still try to have fun. They have spirit. I like this very much.'

'Some of these girls are very beautiful,' considered George. 'But too young.'

The music was very loud and the beer was like a rich reward for all we had come through. I explained to George the strange hybrid called turbofolk, a Serbian fusion of vaguely traditional music with pop instrumentation and thumping beats and lusty lyrics, sung by divas or muscular men. The style had mutated around the Balkans, almost approaching the depths of Eurovision but still too untamed. It was so easy to improve on a bad idea.

Even Macedonia had begun producing its own turbofolk girls (and boys). Ceca, the undisputed queen of the genre and former wife of the late Serbian paramilitary leader Arkan, had purred to the BBC that she was more popular than Madonna in Serbia. It wasn't exactly as earthshaking as when John Lennon had said his little group was more popular than Jesus but it was equally true.

'You know what is strange here,' I said. 'I noticed it from the people at the hotel and the people here. You know when you have a domesticated animal and it goes off in the wild too long, and starts acting like a wild animal? It is like what has happened here.'

'What do you mean?'

'These people were cut off from the outside world for so long, compared to people in Macedonia they are like – wild Macedonians. Their accent, their

67

mannerisms, everything about them … It must be from living under Hoxha for so long and being so isolated. But it is real. They are different.'

Enver Hoxha was the Albanian Communist leader who broke off nearly all contact with the outside world, turning his nation into a sort of lunatic asylum during the Cold War. Obsessed with the idea of foreign invasion, he littered the countryside with concrete bunkers, militarized the borders and shot those who tried to flee. His retarding influence outlived him and has caused Albania to recover from its Communist excesses far more slowly than the other former Communist countries of the Balkans.

Although Communism ended in 1990, five years after Hoxha's death, Albania's Macedonians, mostly clustered in 13 villages on the shores of Lake Prespa, continued to be neglected and forgotten. Whereas the much more numerous Albanian minority in Macedonia had enjoyed major participation at every level of power in the post-Yugoslav state, only in 2005 did the Albanian authorities give the Macedonians of Prespa the right to form a political party.

What was most remarkable, as the disco ball spun and we had another beer, was the visible sexual seg-regation. 'Look,' I said. 'All the boys on one side, all the girls on the other. It's like Texas.'

'It's like Greece – 80 years ago,' said George.

The Pustec zabava was turning out to be truly something and as the night wore on a method emerged from the madness. After an hour, the boys and girls had moved to the long lacquered beer-hall bench in the middle of the room, on their respective sides. Soon enough they were dancing, at first shyly, but then pretty full-on, a spectacle of teenage decadence like anywhere else in the world, to the same songs that were playing at the same time across the water in the republic, in Ohrid and Skopje and Strumica and Stip. I have heard it said that the world, for all its chaos and upheaval, is held together by the prayers of the monks of Mount Athos, on the third finger of Halkidiki, on the other extremity of Macedonia's territory. If not a world, then at least a nation seemed for me, at that moment, to be held together by the iteration of spirit in a lonesome lake village that had somehow preserved its culture despite a malevolent history of arbitrary loss.

It was all too much for me and I was overcome by the conceptual as well as by the alcohol, having eaten nothing since the afternoon. And then there was the dancing, in which George detected a certain philosophy.

It was late, and we got up to go. We were exhausted after the misadventures of the day, and so we left the zabava and headed back to the hotel where the wedding was still roaring, well after three o'clock in the morning.

'Can you imagine?' I said, as we unloaded our bags in the room with no sheets. 'We woke up today in Plati. It seems like a hundred years ago.'

'This was something,' said George, nodding in tired satisfaction. 'Really something.'

Chapter 3

A strong wind greeted us in the morning and for the first time we could see how beautiful the area into which we had fallen by luck or by fate was. The mountain above was steep and solid and it amazed me that we had crossed it. On the left, the lake stretched out from a sandy shore to more hills, behind which must have been the Greek promontory at Psarades where we had been two days earlier. To the north, the water stretched on past the horizon into Macedonia proper.

'How did we *not* fall off that mountain?' I marvelled, looking out from the balcony. George was still too groggy to speak. The water in the bathroom worked, in its own way, and I made my way down the stairs with no rails to where the workmen were dragging heavy tables across the room from the wedding.

I was very hungry and a little bit hung over, but though there had been massive quantities of food the night before, now there was nothing and we had to settle for Turkish coffee. 'It's okay, we will find something to eat up in the village,' I said. 'But let's see the beach before we leave this place.'

It was only a minute's walk to the water's edge across a flat expanse of grass that turned to sand. It lapped evenly and there were small pebbles and a green expanse of reeds to the left, where white egrets or swans stood and poked judgementally in the water with their long slender bills.

The shore where we stood had once been captured by the Greeks, in the Balkan Wars. But later they gave it to Albania and the 13 villages of Mala Prespa ('Little Prespa', as it is known to Macedonians) disappeared, frozen in time, and sucked into the black hole of Enver Hoxha's Albania after World War II. 'Those were not good times for us,' said a man with weathered skin from the hotel, gazing at the sand

and kicking debris. 'Things are getting a little better, though.'

We soon left the hotel and started towards the village. A man in a striped baggy shirt and a train conductor's cap like Bob Dylan might have worn in 1961 saluted us from a ramshackle cart towed by a muscular horse. On the roadside a formidable bonneted old woman foraged with huge bundles of sticks on her back.

By light of day, Pustec was clearly even more extreme than it had seemed the night before. The houses, old and humble in any Macedonian village, were here even more wild and freeform. Behind the crumbling façade of a wall, wooden ribs poked out, long sticks like a wicker basket strung along inside the vanished stone. Very faded block-painted slogans from the Hoxha years crisscrossed old buildings, as did graffiti to American rappers and the local football team.

'This is like something out of a hundred years ago,' I said. 'And think how different it is just over the border!'

'Which border?'

'Any border!'

'Truly remarkable,' George agreed. 'Maybe we can find something to eat?'

We returned to the den of iniquity from the party of the night before in search of fresh meat. The woman at the counter remembered us. 'They have village homemade sausages, fried eggs, bread, things like that,' I told George, as we sat down. The hall looked completely different in the light of day, minus the disco ball and beer-hall benches and carousing teens. The floor was flat and smooth and we waited for the food.

Outside the building there was a miniature dirt football pitch hemmed in by netting. A group of tanned 10-year-old boys were roughhousing and chasing a dog-eaten old football

'How are you guys?' I asked them in Macedonian. 'Pass!'

We played football and they asked many questions about us and why we were there. I was surprised to hear that there were around 100 kids from Pustec and the surrounding area in the school. They learned

Albanian and Macedonian and English. Probably in response to the EU's demands on aspiring members, the Tirana government had allowed the Macedonian flag to fly over the municipal building and the area was officially bilingual.

George, who had undeniable talent with a football, entertained the kids after breakfast and I took the pulse of the locals. An old man who could have been a Highland sheep-owner in a cap and navy sweater sat leaning on the crook of his walking stick on a stone wall.

'Good morning to you,' he said. 'Where do you come from?' he asked.

I introduced ourselves and complemented him on a fine village. He appreciated my interest. After all, if you just went by the name there was little reason for enthusiasm. 'Do you know what "Pustec" means?' he said.

'No, tell me.'

'From the word *"pusto"*, an empty place. They called it like that a long time ago. A place of no worth, with nothing or nobody there.'

'I see. But there are some new houses.' I pointed hopefully at a couple of sleeker and newer constructions and the bright exterior of our makeshift discotheque.

'Yes, some people have money here,' he conceded, but did not tell me how they got it. 'Pustec is the biggest of the Macedonian villages in Little Prespa, like the region's center.'

If Pustec was the most robust, I thought, the others had to be pretty bleak outposts indeed. I told him about our driving misadventures of the night before and the road that just ended. 'Aha, that is the road to Gorica,' he said. 'Not a good road.'

'What are the Macedonian villages here?' I asked.

'Up from here north, you have Sulun, Globocani, Dolna Gorica and Gorna Gorica and then Tuminec before the Macedonian border. Down from here there are Leska, Zrnovsko, Cerje, Rakitsko, Suec and under the very tip of the Small Prespa Lake, Zagradec. All in all, there are 940 people in Pustec, but 4,500 Macedonians in the area.'

It seemed quite a lot, especially when he estimated that were 400 children. 'That is more than in many villages in Macedonia, especially in the east,' I marvelled. Some giggling little girls were watching curiously from the porch of a small shop.

'Yes,' he said. 'I have a Macedonian passport too. Most everyone does.'

I wondered if the straggly folk you saw sometimes in Skopje's open markets selling Albanian olive oil and dried flowers and herbs were from this side of the lake, as I had heard. Only later would I learn about other jobs that had brought labourers from the Albanian side of Prespa to the Macedonian republic.

I bade farewell to the jovial man with the shepherd's crook and found George. We asked for directions and were relieved to find that yes, there was a much better route than the rockslide we had tumbled down the night before. The guide who I would never meet who had been held up on the other side of the border had been right. There was an easier way to get to his village from Greece. There just weren't good signs to tell how it could be done.

77

We rose up higher into the hills and the lake unfolded itself more and more below, the red roofs of Pustec tucked into a protective cove to the left and wild empty fields to the right. The sky was piercingly blue and the water placid, one set of mountains giving way to another as the horizon receded in indigo layers, striated cotton-candy clouds stretched across the upper air. The mountain to the right was reddish and desolate and suddenly they emerged – the concrete bunkers of Enver Hoxha, elliptical and low, like conspiratorial alien pods lying in wait.

'That man was really insane,' pronounced George.

'I would have thought the Albanians would have destroyed them all by now. Wouldn't it embarrass you if this was how your country looked?'

We did not know why the bunkers were still there, though I had heard in some places they had been destroyed. How the dictator had expected they would help in the age of nuclear weapons and air strikes was an even bigger mystery.

Eventually we crossed and started the descent,

where something different began, a long flat plain that marked another environment. The vagaries of politics notwithstanding, the mountain marked the true border between Albania and Macedonia; the population, the nature, the lake, all attested to something that neither isolation nor Communism nor modern politics could kill.

'We did the right thing to go on last night,' said George. 'Yes indeed,' I said. We did not mention how close we were to turning back. But the fact that we had forged on without lights, signs or a map in such conditions led us to agree that we had shown a steely resolve bordering on the British.

The flat road that had seemed so weird and other-worldly the night before just looked underdeveloped in the light of day. The entrance to Korce was long and dusty and the buildings were outdated, but in a different way to the Communist ones of old Yugoslavia or Bulgaria. The houses and shops fronting the street gradually became shinier but at the very center was a roundabout anchored in the middle by a tiny circle of raised concrete, like a bracket on a flat sea, and old and new cars were flying haphazardly around it at various angles and in various directions.

'Which way should we go?' I asked. 'I don't know,' said George, successfully dodging the geometrical traffic. 'Let's park somewhere and walk around.'

We found a place near the experimental roundabout and walked on under huge billowing clouds to where the enormous Orthodox Christian cathedral of Koritsa (as the Greeks call Korce) stood. In southern Albania, just north of Greece, there was a sizeable Orthodox community of Albanians as well as what the Greek government called the 'Greek minority'. The Greek Church played a less direct role in Albanian religious affair than the Greek companies did in the Albanian telecommunications industry, though no less profitable, supporting the Albanian Orthodox Church.

We walked up the long steps and inside. In design it seemed a strange hybrid of the Orthodox and the Catholic (the latter also made up a noticeable part of the Albanian population, along with Muslims), painted with icons but cluttered with long benches.

There were almost no people in the church. A little girl sat in a front pew, head bowed, eyes closed and hands pressed firmly together, a shaft of sunlight coming through a window and the cathedral dust and glancing across her long golden hair.

We went outside of the church and down a tree-lined street where men sold telephone cards from a stool on the sidewalk opposite from an advertisement for a gynaecologist's clinic. A wedding procession was led by a hatchback wreathed in flowers and George noticed that the public buses were Greek ones, but taken out of service there long ago. 'They must have been donated,' he said.

It soon became undeniable that the women of Korce had much more going for them than the men. While the latter's rough desultory loitering was far from the gallant brawny soldiers depicted on an old Communist war memorial we passed, the women seemed to pay genuine attention to appearances and 'even how they walk,' said George. 'Painful! You don't even see such things so much anymore in Greece.'

Where their elegant clothes came from, however,

was a mystery as the shop windows of the town center were crowded with bland and bizarre monotone garments. 'These clothes are from the 1950s!' lamented the Greek. 'Horrible!' Outside a newspaper shop further along two women were waiting to pay to weigh themselves on scales.

We stopped at an outdoor café under high umbrellas to plan the rest of our afternoon. For me, there was nothing as calming as having a coffee when planning something, or thinking about how or even whether to plan something, or simply enjoying the day. I had heard that in America many intelligent adults were using cafés as places of business when they had laptops but no jobs. There and in England I knew for a fact that in cafés people read books by themselves, and even when there were many other people around to talk to. I was glad not to be a part of all that.

'We will see right now,' I said, as the serving boy came with a full tray.

He set them down. 'See!' I said. 'A macchiato like we have in Macedonia. Why don't they do this in Thessaloniki?'

After the Greek, the Turkish and the French coffees, the macchiato was the next point of confusion. In Greece when I ordered such a thing they would eventually bring a half-full cup of espresso with a dash of milk. Yet in Macedonia, as had occurred now in Korce, you would get the espresso but with more milk, and culminating in a whipped foamy head. You could stir it and add sugar and the cups frequently had Italian names embedded in them.

'Aha, I see,' said George, sizing up the drink. 'This is a mistake. They *do* do it correctly in Greece. "Macchiato" comes from the Italian verb *macchiare*, "to stain" – which is what happens to the surface of the espresso when you add just a little milk.'

George's grammar was impeccable. We had been living an illusion in Macedonia and, it appeared in Albania, at least in this café.

'Then what would you call "our" macchiato?' I asked.

'A *café au lait.*'

'Yes, you are right,' I conceded. 'Just be careful if you order a Frappé in Macedonia. It's not like in

83

Greece, with whipped Nescafe in water or milk. It's something with banana. It's absolutely disgusting.'

'What do I have to say to get a real Frappé, then?'

'A Café Nes,' I said. 'Better yet, order "iced coffee". That is a Frappé, but with ice cream.'

Coffee in the Balkans was serious stuff, and so was work. George's work at the university had been interrupted by yet another strike by the students.

'Is it just me, or do the Greek students go on strike every year when the weather is nice?'

'Greek students are just terrible,' grumbled George. 'They are the world's last Leninists.'

I burst out laughing and he continued.

'They expect the state to pay for their housing, their insurance, indefinitely, while they sit in Kamara all day and drink coffee!' he said. 'This latest strike, where they protested and shut down the universities, occurred because the government wanted to pass an educational reform law to put some rational limits on the number of years you can spend as an undergraduate. There is almost no limit.'

'Really!'

'It is ridiculous. Where else do you find 34-year-old undergraduates?' George was getting animated. The whole concept was very funny, and very true.

'The Greek student mentality,' he continued, 'is that just having a degree should guarantee you a job after you graduate. Boys! The world is a very competitive place! No one will hire you without skills!'

I knew some Greek professors who were not industrious like George and I suspected that the lethargy was not one-sided.

'Yes,' said George. 'The worst thing is that there is this secret student-professor complicity behind all these strikes. Neither group wants to do any work, so they are both happy when the university is closed.'

In 1974, after the fall of the hard-line military junta in Athens, a university asylum law was passed. Police would no longer be allowed onto any university campus without a special permit from the rector.

'This was originally passed to protect the students from police brutality,' said George. 'But things have changed – students now can sell drugs in the university and the police can't do anything. Three weeks in a row, there was an anonymous bomb threat against a university library, and they closed everything down. It turned out the guy who made the threat just didn't want to have to go to class on those days.'

We left the café and Korce soon after and were back on the main road heading north to Pogradec, on the southern shore of Lake Ohrid. This, the largest of the three Macedonian lakes, lay under Mount Galicica through which it was fed by underground springs from Prespa on the other side. Tectonic crunching and glacial scraping had created this unique geography of deep aqueous basins and high peaks and as we drove north the far-off mountain ridge with which we had battled the night before ran parallel with us.

The Albanian plain, however, was a different world entirely, fields of grass and tall sunflowers and women in wide-brimmed hats tending them, while on the side of the old road we passed more and more onions in red netted bags. Some of them were on proper stands with other produce, but most were just thrown together and watched over by a child or old man and no cars stopped to buy any of them.

Eventually the road climbed and became more forested and then we reached the top and started the descent into Pogradec. It was a small town that was rapidly growing and, it seemed, in all the wrong ways. The center was congested and afflicted with the kind of gauche modern buildings that had become ever more common in Albanian-inhabited parts of western Macedonia. Also in Pogradec was the first graffiti for the UCK, the former 'Kosovo Liberation Army' paramilitaries that fought the Serbs with air support from NATO in 1999. The popularity of such irredentists had not been evident in Korce or along the way and it was a sign that we were getting closer to Macedonia.

'This town is very ugly,' I said. 'I did not expect this.'

'Shall we continue then?' said George. 'Along the lake?'

'Yes, let us see what there is.'

The lake road branched off to the right from

another one that passed further north and then west to Tirana. Pogradec was very close to one Macedonia border crossing, at Sveti Naum a couple of kilometres to the east, but we wanted to follow the lake along its north-western shore towards the border crossing of Kafasan, to make the eventual circle around it.

Like Prespa, Ohrid had been divided; one-third to Albania, and two-thirds to Yugolsav Macedonia. Unlike on the Albanian-controlled bank of Prespa, there were actually Albanians living in the few villages along the way. However, neither they nor their government had succeeded in repairing the damage done by Enver Hoxha and his military-industrial complexes.

'Look, there's a rusted train track on the lake front,' I said. 'Oh, and some bunkers on the water. Nice touch.'

'What do you suppose they were doing?'

'I have heard there are some coal deposits or something in the hills near the lake,' I said.

'But the bunkers are really too much.'

'It was in case the Macedonians invaded by submarine. Got to be ready for anything, you know.'

We passed by very small villages though there was nothing intriguing about them and the drive was not helped by the unhappy grey clouds that cast a pallor over everything. But I was especially sad when I saw the fish.

'What has he got there?' said George, looking at a teenage boy shouting and waving a line on which flopped a very unfortunate dying fish.

'It is an Ohrid trout,' I said. 'An endangered species that is unique to this lake. And the kid is just standing there selling them.'

Everyone knew that the laws and bi-national conventions were disregarded, but this display seemed especially blatant. The fact that Macedonia and Albania shared the lake made environmental cooperation impossible. Macedonia blamed Albania for dynamite-fishing the trout and for failing to go along with the moratorium the Skopje government had passed on fishing.

Nevertheless, it was hypocritical of the Macedonian government, I explained to George, to ban the fishing of the trout but not the selling of it. The police would

89

crack down by making an example of some fisherman out in his canoe, but at the same time do nothing when every restaurant in Ohrid was plainly advertising and serving the endangered and expensive trout.

'I asked a local why this was once,' I said, 'and he told me, "Hey, politicians have to eat too, you know".'

Still, in Macedonia you did not see boys waving fish in front of you on the side of the road. On the other hand, the Albanian-controlled side seemed to have preserved more of the reed belts vital to the survival of the trout and other species – probably due to the fact that a rusting train track ran along the shore and tourism was limited.

There were a few places, however, and George suggested the option of stopping at one for the night. We passed by them infrequently and they were very small and set apart from other life. Some hotels had extensions built out over the water. But they were inevitably blighted by the same sham modernity as Pogradec and big black cars with Kosovo license plates stood outside. 'I think you get more than a bed and a meal in that one,' I remarked. 'It's not that late yet. Maybe the next villages will be more interesting.'

So we continued on and the road went up and away from the lake, and on the top we could see a settlement down on the water.

'Shall we see what's there?'

'All right.'

Lin was the last village before the border and it had retained more of its character than the other lake settlements that had preceded it. We parked in front of a building that read 'Hotel', where boys congregated in groups in the dirt. One narrow street passed into the village and it divided the half that was on the lake from the half that was not. Trellises ran across it in places and old stone houses, or bright blue houses, and in front of one red peppers were drying on a white cloth on the ground.

The side lanes perpendicular to the water were tiny and led into a warren of tightly-packed low houses and in the closed yards women sat fixing things or preparing things. Down one wider lane an old woman in a black cloak stood inside a wire fence speaking to her neighbours on the shore. The lakefront properties here were shacks with cor- rugated-iron walls and on the ground was chick- enfeed and tires for burning. Behind them was a gleaming minaret. A sign on the mosque in Arabic and Albanian stated that it had been built in 2001 by the United Arab Emirates. Further on, where the village ended, a similarly new church stood but there was no explanation for its more mysterious presence in the Muslim Albanian village.

Lin was a place of closed walls and closed stares and it was only funny for a moment when an impish little boy ran up to play a trick on an old man and the latter became very angry and started chasing the boy to hit him with his stick. But except for that, there was nothing, and in light of the way that the locals lived on the lake without any apparent appreciation for it beyond washing buckets, the existence of a hotel seemed like just a bad joke.

'Let's go,' I said. 'Let's get to Macedonia. I have a good plan.'

'Okay, boy. So then we go.'

To tell the truth, I was homesick. I missed Macedonia and there were things there that could not be missed. George only had a few more days before returning to his university, and I did not want to waste time where there was nothing to waste it on.

At the border the Albanian guards tested George's patience by running an auction on the alleged vehicle tax he had to pay to get out of the country. Watching him from the car as he gesticulated at the police, I was praying that he wouldn't cause an 'incident' when we were so close to getting out.

'They were very illogical,' he fumed when they finally waved us through. 'I doubt if that vehicle tax even exists!'

From Kafasan we entered Macedonia on the straight road to Struga and I was very happy. Down below to our right was the lake again, gently arcing towards the east. After 15 minutes we arrived in Struga, where the air was always more soft and rich than anywhere else on the lake. We parked near the center and the smooth stone of the wide pedestrian street in the old town was wet from a shower that had just passed. But the town's real miracle was its river, the Crn Drim, which somehow maintained its course and speed as it ran under the surface of the lake from the exact opposite side, at Sveti Naum near Pogradec, tumbling out into Struga and running up through western Macedonia and into Lake Debar.

We had coffee again in the old town. I was pleased to again be vindicated in error by ordering a macchiato and getting what was really a café au lait. The street was crowded with life; ladies with shopping bags, foreign tourists in baggy shorts and young women in miniskirts, skull-capped old Albanian men, a bearded Wahhabi Muslim or two and tables where local vendors sold their wares.

Struga was not large and as evening grew closer we had reached the waterfront. Unlike most of the beaches to the south in Ohrid town and further on, Struga boasted sand, and the shallowness of the water here also made it very warm. And, while environmentalists complained that some reed belts had been destroyed by the residents in local Albanian-populated villages, the aquatic foliage had survived here better than in the more southerly shores of the lake, where the bulk of Ohrid's hotels were.

We crossed the lake road and came onto the beach. Before us, at the water's edge, an old man stood silhouetted in darkness, leaning on his cane and gazing out across the rippling water that filled the vague and enormous hemisphere before all. It was a moment of extreme sensitivity and I could not describe it and I was very happy later on when the picture that I took then came out right, and I could see that I wouldn't have to explain anything more than the picture did.

Below a patio café some boys were playing table tennis beside the beach and we watched them with great interest as they laughed and dived and sliced. George was very keen on the sport and after a few rounds one of the boys won out and George took a turn on the table against him. Then he graciously bowed out and we thanked them and got in the car to go to Vevchani.

'You are going to love this village,' I said. 'It is really one of the very best places in Macedonia.'

There was no place in the country like it. After

Macedonia became independent in 1992, the village threatened it would declare itself an independent republic: the well-kept Orthodox Christian Macedonian stronghold was situated unpromisingly near the mountain border with Albania, between Albanian and Macedonian Muslim villages with criminal and radical elements. But Vevchani did not share the politically-correct appeasement tendencies of the country as a whole and, unlike other Macedonian villages that died out through emigration or political submission it was not prepared to sacrifice its way of life, its religion or its traditions.

Among the latter was the masked winter carnival, which took place every January on the Orthodox New Year (according to the old Julian Calendar), on January 13th and 14th. I had been to the Vevchani Carnival a couple of years previous, and since then I had written plenty of articles about the place. As a republic in spirit if not in fact, Vevchani printed its own passports and currency, the *lichnik*, which was very colourful and ran from the 50 to the 1,000, the illustrations ranging, in order of value, from the mayor's visage on the smallest to naked women on the most valuable.

We arrived there after a 20-minute drive from Struga, passing the small church under pines where the first houses were. Up above in the open center of the village a new Greek amphitheatre had been built and spring water poured from a ledge like a waterfall. When digging for the amphitheatre, workmen had discovered foundation stones for an old church that had been forgotten underground; it dated at least to 1895, when a commemorative stone from the wicked Sultan Abdul Hamid found there had been inscribed; but some archaeologists conjectured it might have been built over a much older Roman-era church. Then there was the peculiar business of a triangular ornament discovered behind where the priests would have stood and there was talk of Masonic influence. Anything was possible in Vevchani.

'They told me that even the old people forgot this church was there,' I said, as we clambered over the partially excavated ruins. 'Even though they took big stones from the demolished church to build their own houses.'

'Remarkable,' said George.

With its pristine natural setting, roaring springs and history, Vevchani was a promising tourist destination but the ornery locals had still not latched onto the concept of foreign marketing. But the World Bank and a European foundation had donated towards a small pensione, the Kutmichevitsa, which had two rooms done up in traditional style with village bedspreads and fireplaces and a perfect view over the plain to Lake Ohrid down below. I had wanted to stay there but it was full. So we took private accommodation with Liljana, a woman who worked for the municipality, and her family in their three-floor ancestral palace near a 19th-century church. It was a common custom in Macedonia for several generations of a family to share a house of several floors. Those who were tourism-minded might have several rooms free in summer and the price was eminently sound at only 5 euros a head.

Liljana remembered me and was delighted to see us. She was from a Serbian background and had that wonderfully alive Serbian way of communicating, with vivid arm gestures and open eyes and laughter. Her husband was a Vevchani man and the grandmother of the house sat in her shawl and the daughters, 21-year-old Bojana and Jovana, six years younger, sat at the table in the kitchen with us.

'She asks if you want sugar in your coffee,' I said.

'*Da, da*,' affirmed an attentive and smiling George. He was in a certain situation where he felt the vague overlap between the beginner's Russian that he had learned in England and Macedonian might be useful.

The grandmother carefully sized up the Greek as if she were judging ripe produce. 'Is he married?' I translated again.

'Ha! What is this?' laughed George. 'What a question!' He had already complemented the mother on the beauty of her daughters. Everyone loved George, who was unfailingly polite and sweet with his Slavic phrases. Then we were shown our room which was on the top floor and had a very large balcony. From it you could see the tiled rooftops of the houses clustered below and the mountain to the right, Jablanica, which ran like a spine up the western border with Albania.

After hot showers we were finally ready to go and eat. Although there was no room at the inn, it had a little restaurant with great rustic appeal and, I remembered, great ribs. 'The least we can do is eat there,' I said.

'All right boy,' said George, who had taken out a very nice shirt for the first time. 'We will go out tonight in Struga,' I said.

Downstairs we said goodbye to Liljana and announced we were going out for the evening. 'Don't worry, the door will be unlocked,' she said and laughed at our washed and half-decent attire. 'You are going out to work something!'

'What did she mean?' pondered George, when we were out walking up the narrow street where a old cherry-red Serbian car was parked under fertile trees.

'What do you think?' I said.

'Boy! I'm very hungry,' pronounced the Greek. 'We deserve a good meal.'

Eating at a table on the balcony of the pensione was a group of men including Vasil the mayor, who greeted us heartily. I had written plenty of times about the village and the new pensione after it had been established and my Vevchani passport bore the mayor's signature. I could not understand all of the villagers' inscrutable ways but in some sense I still felt like an honorary citizen.

'Come to my office tomorrow morning if you are free,' said the mayor.

'All right!'

We admired the view from the balcony. It was dark and the lights of Ohrid town far away twinkled low and even. Then the call to prayer started up from a mosque. Just below Vevchani was Oktisi, populated mostly by Macedonian Muslims, the Torbeshi, a small minority who, like other Slavic Muslims in Bosnia and Bulgaria, had converted to Islam during the Ottoman era. The name came from the Macedonian word *torba* ('bag') and it was not especially flattering; according to one explanation, the insinuation was that those people would follow any creed or any order if the master would fill their bags with goods.

But there was something to it as the Torbeshi had proved extraordinarily fickle in their political allegiances, supporting ethnically Macedonian parties, then Albanian ones, depending on who might serve their interests better. In fairness, they had long been alienated due to their odd combination of Macedonian ethnicity and language and Muslim religion. Most recently this ostracisation had driven some of the bag men into the arms of the Arabs and now you could find Islamic fundamentalists with long beards in the Muslim villages around – paid, allegedly, by foreign interests to bring the look and feel of Saudi Arabia or Pakistan to the heart of the Balkans. They didn't pose much of a threat, yet, but it was another reason for the Vevchani people to be glad to own a gun.

The Kutmichevitsa had a hunting lodge atmosphere, with heavy wooden tables and well-built country men drinking and grotto walls of rough stone illuminated from small apertures like in a crypt. We ordered big bottles of beer and hunter's *pleskavica*, a thick plain hamburger with yellow cheese and spices inside. 'Very good indeed,' George said. 'This is very nourishing food.'

George had already tried, on a previous trip, the Macedonian national salad, *sopska salata*, with tomatoes and cucumbers and soft white cheese on top and to this we added *nafura*, the lovely crunchy fried bread with the same cheese in fluffy pieces crowning it. Somehow the cumulative effect of salt and red pepper and oil from the grill gave the bread an evanescent sweetness as baffling as the Ohrid Eel, said to migrate from the Sargasso Sea through the ocean and through streams to reach the lake.

The dinner was leisurely and long and we ordered another beer, allowing time to digest and take stock of what we had done. George was pleasantly surprised with what we had found and I told him the village would be even better during the day. 'Do you want to see what we can see in Struga?' I said. 'It is a Monday night so I don't know if there is anything happening, but we can see.'

We finished and thanked the gracious proprietor,

who apologized again for not having had a free room. 'I gave it away just three hours before you came,' he said. Yet it had worked out all right: I always liked to see Liljana, and her smiling daughters were, I could tell, raising the status of the country in George's eyes far better than any diplomat could.

In Struga, we parked near the river that tumbled out of the lake. Over it was the bridge, the gently rising romantic one where the poetry festival began every August. For almost 50 years poets from the region and from around the world, some famous ones too, came to give homage to tradition of Constantin Miladinov, the 19th-century poet who wrote lovingly of his home while living in Russia, in a poem entitled *T'ga za Jug* ('Longing for the South'). This melancholic reminiscence was one of Macedonia's national lyrics; in it, the poet laments the cold and frost of Russia and begs for wings to fly back to the warmth of Struga on the life-giving lake.

On the opposite bank were a string of small bars and they had music coming from them but not so many people inside. 'What can we expect?' said

George. 'After all, it is Monday.' But it was not just that. August was also fading, and with it the tourist season. Macedonians had a firmly ingrained sense of summer vacation as executable strictly between the middle of July and the middle of August. Things were thus more peaceful immediately before and after those days, and the water was still warm for swimming.

After a beer in Struga we decided to head back for one more in Vevchani and then call it a night. It was hard to believe that we had woken up that morning amidst windy mountains in Pustec. It was an entire world, an entire century away. George was stoic but tired after constant driving since 'Saloniki and we needed a rest.

Vevchani's nightspot had once been in the lower village, but someone had had the good sense to move it up above the church, closer to the gushing springs in the forest which were lit and which had wooden benches along spacious paths where young couples went to kiss at night.

The bar was small but the youths in windbreakers were satisfied and so were we. An American disaster movie with Croatian subtitles played on TV and we sipped Bulgarian beer. There was laughter and a relaxed confidence in this village that, while in some ways just an enclave like Pustec, was more flourishing and self-assured and eternal in a way that gave you hope for the future rather than in a way that made you believe in the miracle of survival in a country of old men. Two experiences, but one nation, the songs playing were the same, and it was time for us to sleep with the sound of water rushing from above and the young in one another's arms returning out of the darkness down the sylvan path of late summer.

Chapter 4

The roosters started in before dawn and by early morning Vevchani was alive with the sound of wood-chopping and little kids running around, though the marbled clouds in the mountains indicated that the day was still trying to decide what to do with itself.

Liljana had already gone to work in the old municipal building and so we had coffee again with the grandmother of the house. She spoke animatedly about the village carnival and other things, and satisfied the philosopher's wish to learn more about the village with a guided tour by young Bojana who graciously agreed, even though she was still in bed when she was asked. George had a cold shower again and we set off still hungry, but clean. Across from us on the right was the Church of St. Nikola. It had been built in 1876 and boasted a great collection of icons.

In the entrance there was a small window where a young woman was selling wax candles and guarding the church. In the spring she had sold me a red candle shaped like an Easter egg. Neither was expensive, though the four-foot-tall spiralling white ones that looked like rockets were.

The woman had dark hair and dark eyes and she was from somewhere else. She had married a man from Vevchani and settled down there and I had never met anyone else who gave more attention to dusting and cleaning a church. She took it seriously and turned on the lights so that we could see the ornate furnishings and icons and wall paintings but photos were not allowed.

The church was typical Byzantine-style Orthodox, with alcoves along the sides lined with icons and an ornamented mount in the middle for the officiating priest, behind the iconostasis, the hidden place where only priests and other men could go. The oldest icon was Russian and from the 18th century, and some of them were printed in Greek letters but most in Church Slavonic. 'This is a very nice church,' said George. 'Is the priest here?' I asked. He was quite a character but he would not be in until later so we said we would come back.

'The air is so clean here!' marvelled George as we walked up the steep lane leading to the springs. 'Very invigorating. It heightens your senses and your appetites. I really ate a lot last night because of this atmosphere.'

We soon reached the entrance to the springs, where the path went up through the forest and over the first wooden bridge. 'Let us see if this church is open,' said Bojana, looking at a tiny chapel to the left. It was. Inside the humble enclosure stood a few icons, sand in a tray for candles and a musty smell due to the dampness in the air.

Ice-cold water running down from Jablanica fed the springs of Vevchani and, when the former Yugoslav authorities had sought to dam it for power generation, the villagers rebelled, even using old ladies as 'human shields'. In the end, the Belgrade authorities had to give up. 'You can drink the water,' said Bojana. 'It's very clean.'

With a cupped hand the philosopher drank from the sparkling stream where mosses and clover clung to smooth rocks. The onrushing water was never the same twice and in every place it was different too. The water was at its highest level in spring, after the melting winter snows unleashed frigid torrents, but because it was the end of summer now it was less and more of the accompanying greenness was exposed. The smooth wood of curling soft-leaved trees hung protectively over the water which formed in foam-flecked eddies and pools over submerged roots and copper and bronze lichenous stone, and stone made of a metal which does not exist in this world, or at least no longer. It was like something that had been written in an ancient Greek pastoral idyll and I suspected that the votive shrines around the banks of the springs probably had pagan roots, like the Vevchani carnival itself.

On the other side of the water from the little chapel was another, slightly larger one, with ornate wood-carvings inside. 'Macedonian religious art is most famous for its wood carving,' I said to George. 'If we go to Debar sometime, to Sveti Bigorski Monastery, you will see there a twenty-foot-high iconostasis carved in three dimensions with millions of intricate details. I think it is as incredible as any art you can find in the Western world.'

Outside the chapel was a small shrine where thin wax candles were neatly stacked next to icons of saints and the wax-covered raised metal bowl where people offered prayers and lit them. In antiquity such things perhaps existed in the form of cults to a woodland goddess, perhaps Artemis, and later those of the Slav tribes. A branch of the Via Egnatia, the famed Roman road that went east-west across the south Balkans, passed nearby Vevchani. Things reappeared; sometimes a coin turned up, or a statue of a horse for a doorstep or, as we had seen, an entire substructure of a church.

'There is really something in the air here,' remarked George after we had climbed upwards and down again. 'Can we go in there?'

He was pointing to a cave-liked opening which stood at the base of the springs. It was very dark and you could not see the back of it and the rocks hung over the top at rough angles.

'Sure,' said Bojana.

He turned on his camera. 'Would you mind taking a picture of us?'

'No problem.'

George and I clambered down into the cave, hopping from one stone to another across the water and positioned ourselves against the walls for a photo. It was not very deep but the walls were covered with a kind of inland algae and I was disappointed not to see frescoes.

'I'm surprised. This would make a perfect monastic grotto,' I thought aloud. 'Or maybe the water is too high in spring.'

We left the springs and the moist, dizzying air and continued our tour through the upper part of the village. On the side of the street were slight culverts through which spring water was channelled. Slovenian and Macedonian beer cooled in a red bottle-rack in one of them and they were clean and not sullied with trash as was the case in Labunishta, a Muslim village also tucked into the mountain to the north. 'The unique thing about this place is that the people have taken care of it,' I said to George. 'If every village in Macedonia was like this, it would be an absolute paradise.'

The road curved around the well-maintained stone houses where tiny old Zastavas and Ladas were parked and Bojana led us into a small open building where a workman stood atop a rickety contraption of wooden planks and chains and he was feeding grain into a chute that emptied into a pot inside a bigger one. The millstone was grinding it into flour and everything around was covered in fine white powder.

'This is the traditional way of making flour,' said Bojana. We introduced ourselves to the man, Branko, who wore a long blue shirt and spectacles. I thought it must be very hard to not get flour on them but he seemed to be doing well enough. 'I have been doing this for twelve years,' he told us.

'How much flour do you make here?' I asked.

'Enough for the village!' He was filling large sacks with the flour.

'Do they sell it? Do people pay for it?'

'I am not sure but I think it is collective,' said the girl, 'and nobody pays.'

Flour-for-free seemed like a real bonus and we were getting to like this village more and more. There was even, finally, a souvenir shop that had been created at some point that year and I bought George a Vevchani passport in case he ever returned at carnival time.

Before we left the village we stopped in at the church again to see the priest, Zoran, who had arrived in the meantime. He was genial and offered us *rakija*, or raki as it was known to George, the fiery Balkan liqueur concocted from beaten and abused grapes. We said cheers to Greece and to Macedonia and to Vevchani and the priest took us from his office and up a stair into the church to a level I had not seen before. 'We would like to make an icon gallery with these pieces,' he said earnestly. 'You know we have some here that are quite old.'

'Real treasures,' said George. 'I am surprised –

114

nobody would expect in some small village like this to have such things!'

But that was the magic of Vevchani, and before we left I wanted to spend a moment with the mayor as he had invited us to stop by. The municipal building was an imposing old structure from Communist times, or maybe even earlier, the only such building in the village, and it was located in the very center of Vevchani near the parking lot and the school and the Greek amphitheatre. We went up the stairs and were soon shown into Vasil's office and seated on comfortable couches.

'Welcome back!' he said. 'What will you have to drink?'

We had coffee with the mayor and George complemented him on the fine time he had had in the village. 'We will try to bring him back for the carnival,' I said. I added that I was impressed how the village seemed to be improving in some small way every year. 'Except the kids sometimes break the lights in the springs,' he said.

'You know what Vevchani needs to go with the winter carnival,' I said. 'A Summer Olympics.'

The mayor laughed. 'It could be something with feats of strength and three-legged races and alcohol,' I continued. 'Sort of a mirror-image of the winter madness.'

He filed away my suggestion and we talked some more about our trip and the book I would write and I left a copy of a magazine article I had written about Vevchani. 'Thank you very much for this,' he said, 'and good luck with the rest of your trip.'

We said goodbye to him and to our hosts and reluctantly left the idyllic village at the foot of the lush mountain. I had gotten word that my wife and small son were on their way from Skopje to Ohrid by bus and we had to get there to meet them. I also phoned an archaeologist who I knew in the town, Pasko Kuzman at the Ohrid Museum. I had a feeling there would be a great meeting of minds between him and the Greek philosopher and I hoped that Pasko would have time to show us the secret treasures of Ohrid's gold and jewels at some point in the next couple of days.

'What does he say?' asked George, as we were

driving back towards Struga and the road that carried on to Ohrid.

'He says we should show up this afternoon and he can show us the museum. I explained that you aren't here for much longer.'

'Excellent!'

We were hungry when we arrived in Ohrid and after parking near the old town we began to forage. 'Let us have *burek*,' I said. 'It will be enough to hold you until dinner.'

'What is burek?' said George.

'It is something like a *tyropita*, but not exactly. It is this crunchy filo pie with white cheese, or ground beef if you want. It is Turkish in origin and the dough is crunchy but fairly soft on the inside.'

'I see.'

'I think you will like it, anyway I will have one.'

Burek was really an institution in Macedonia, as elsewhere in the Balkans but better, I thought, than in Turkey where it was too soft. It was inevitably served on a thin scratched metal plate and eaten with knife and fork, and best at breakfast though it could be handy throughout the day or when there was extra alcohol in the blood to be soaked up.

'This is not bad,' said George. We were sitting in the small shop next to the big glass case where the round trays of burek lay. We had yoghurt, that is, drinkable yoghurt, the usual accompaniment to burek and many other foods in Macedonia.

After we ate we traipsed through the long stone streets of the old town, past Ohrid's distinctive white, wood-framed buildings and Byzantine churches. Despite the ambivalent weather there were plenty of locals and tourists out and the cafés were busy.

As we approached the museum we caught sight of a man rushing towards us, white beard flying and spectacles bouncing on his nose. It was Pasko.

'I am sorry, but I was called to go out now. Can you come tonight, to the museum?'

'Sure, what time?'

'Come at nine o'clock,' said the archaeologist, and, apologizing again, rushed off.

'Maybe it's better,' said George. 'We will have more time then.'

'Now what do we do?'

'We can have a coffee until their bus comes. Did you find your friend about the accommodation for tonight?' said George.

'Daniel? Yes, he is here. Maybe he will join us for coffee.'

We sat outside on the main square near where the boats were docked on the vast lake and where the busy wide pedestrian street lined with shops began. We had the third coffee of the day and waited for Daniel to arrive. He was a local friend of mine originally from a village further south on the lake coast, and he said his father could rent us a room there for as long we needed. He had just got married and had a small baby and when he finally arrived he had the same impish yet hurried look, like he was planning something but did not have much time, and a staccato speech that was impossible not to mimic.

'Chris! How are you?'

'Dan-iel! We are good.'

George said hello and offered his sincere thanks once again. George was the godfather of my son and when he had been in Ohrid the summer before for the baptism, we had parked his car one night in a place that turned out to be illegal. It disappeared and luckily Daniel, who had just left us a few minutes before, volunteered to come with us through a variety of police stations and car pounds where we had to fill out multiple forms and pay numerous fees to recover the car, which had indeed been stolen by the police.

'Women here are very beautiful,' remarked George.

'Oof. Yes they are,' said Daniel.

'How was the summer?' I asked. 'A lot of tourists?' I knew that he had gone into business with another local man engaged in importing Dutch tourists.

'Yes. Very many tourists. There were new charter flights. Too much work. And you? How is your trip going?'

We told him about our adventures between Greece and Albania and he said that actually that very night he would be going to Albania for a seaside holiday. Suddenly that summer Albanian tour operators had turned to the Macedonian market, and many people we knew had gone or were going on package tours to the coast, in resorts near Vlore or Drach. 'It is very cheap,' said Daniel. 'They make good business also because Macedonians need a visa to go to places like Greece and Croatia.'

Daniel had studied Macedonian philology at university in Skopje. He was an expert on issues of language and had some interesting views on history and we started talking about things. I brought up how a man in Vevchani had provoked George about Alexander the Great and how the latter had tactfully spoken of 'our mutual heritage'. But there was no need for him to apologize.

'All these approaches through a constructed past,' said George, 'leave no way for history to be approached objectively.'

'I agree,' said Daniel. 'It is very stupid.'

We continued talking for a few minutes and then my wife called. 'They are almost here,' I said. 'Shall we go?'

We went to the bus station, which had been moved from its old town-center location in order to ease congestion. Now it was just outside of Ohrid, being little more than a small office set on a long expanse of tar.

After a few minutes the bus arrived and through the crowds dismounted a slim Macedonian woman with black hair and a chunky, blonde stand-up infant.

'Wow!' exclaimed George, who hadn't seen Marco in a year. 'What do we have here? This is a real *boy*!'

Marco looked disoriented and just stood there, the way he always did when seeing people he felt strongly about after a long absence. George threw him up in the air in his arms and the real boy was soon smiling.

'*Koj e?*' ('Who is he?'), prompted my wife.

'*Kum Tzorge*' ('Godfather George'), said Marco with satisfaction.

We went with Daniel to say hello to his wife and he gave us the directions to Pestani. It was a village 20 minutes away down the coast. To get there we passed out of the town and past a string of hotels, most of them imposing and dating from Yugoslav times and then thick forests, only occasionally broken up by small villages. Sometimes you could see the lake around a bend or through the trees and sometimes you could not.

Daniel's father was an energetic, balding man and he greeted us with vigorous handshakes and showed us to the rooms where we unloaded our things. The family house was down a side lane adjacent to a large hotel, the Desaret, which took its name from an ancient Macedonian tribe that had inhabited the area over two millennia ago. Our host told us that we could get dinner there, as well as in Pestani, which was itself a long village directly on the lake with a long beach, which made it a favourite destination for holiday-makers, both young people and families, and it was always crowded during the high season. But things had quieted down now, and many of the restaurants and shops – which were not so many to begin with – had shut for the season. Yet we found one that had grilled meat and fish and a patio with winding flowers and booming Macedonian music.

Everyone was full of questions for everyone else,

especially my wife, for the guest of honour. 'George, how are you?' she said. 'How is Neni? How is your mother? I want to know everything!' She was very lively, sometimes too much, but had a very good heart and communicated very clearly. She had been sure that it would be an impossible task to keep a small bear, as we referred to Marco, happy on a long, hot bus ride and to deal with him for what would be weeks of travel. But as I had expected, once they had successfully arrived everything was different.

George gave an account of the trips he had made recently to foreign countries, which she liked hearing about very much, as well as his work, and then his relationships, which she liked hearing about even more. 'That Neni is so nice!' said my wife. 'She is such an honest and good person. I wish she came with you.'

'Yes, well I'm sure she wishes that too,' said George. 'But she had to work. She sends her greetings to you and to this – I don't even know what to call him! I mean, he is just a massive boy!'

'That's our bear,' said Buba with a smile. Marco

weighed around 16 kilos and was a couple of months shy of his second birthday. Now he was busy stabbing fried potatoes in ketchup and putting them in his mouth, sometimes successfully. He had the same love of eating as I did and blue eyes like me but the gentle Macedonian curve under the eyebrows where his nose began. All in all he was a very lovely boy who had been very popular the summer before on the lake shore with older women, particularly the seven- to nine-year-old set. With the same irrational optimism of all parents we imagined he would be a star someday. He loved being the center of attention and George, who like every good Mediterranean man took his role as godfather very seriously, was giving him plenty of it.

After dinner we left Buba to put Marco to bed and headed back into Ohrid to finally meet Pasko Kuzman. We found him sitting outside a café with a silver-haired Romanian couple who were introduced to us as poets. I did not know where he found such people but all things considered it did not surprise me.

Pasko was a great man who clearly loved his work. He had multiple diving watches running up his wrists, long white hair and a white beard, wire-rimmed spectacles and jovial red cheeks – a cross between Santa Claus and Indiana Jones.

We walked up the old streets of Ohrid and into the stately museum, and then up the long stairs to a workshop where shelves were lined with artefacts and a long table stood in the center with special lights and drawings and books. It was clearly the place that Pasko loved most and he began leisurely showing us around the collection, which dated from the ancient Macedonian period to the medieval Slavic and Byzantine, everything in it having been found in Ohrid and its surrounding villages.

George was overwhelmed. 'This is really amazing,' he said. 'I did not expect to find such things here.'

There was a row of ancient helmets with rams' horns where the ear guards were and small golden squares with the 16-rayed Sun of Vergina, the famous emblem of the ancient house of Macedon which had caused so much trouble when the modern republic had chosen it for its national flag. After hysterical protests and an embargo from Greece, the country changed the flag, as well as the currency and even the constitution. The sun also featured on the bottom of a rounded vessel. 'This was for drinking wine,' said Pasko. On the table were careful coloured-pencil sketches in a folded-out book of records of the pieces that had been found. 'Such items tell us that ancient Ohrid, then called Lychnidos, was a Macedonian city after all.'

'Really!' said George.

'In the Yugoslav times, we were taught in school that it had been an Illyrian city – this was due to Tito's anti-nationalism policy. But the archaeological records show that it was an ancient Macedonian city, and an important one. We are also planning to excavate in a hill near Ohrid, where it is likely that another city of Philip II of Macedon was located.'

All of this was very exciting for George, who was interested not only in ancient philosophy but in literature and culture and all of the marks of the bygone worlds of the ancient Mediterranean. We were shown a very heavy statue of Hercules, earrings in the shape of a boy riding a golden dolphin with ruby eyes and finally the golden mask of Trebenista – an ancient Macedonian burial site found in the village of the same name.

'There were others found here, but they were taken by the Bulgarians and Serbs during and after the wars,' said Pasko. 'This is the only such mask left in Macedonia.' He had discovered it a few years earlier, along with a golden glove, and the discovery had caused a sensation in the country. It was pale, fragile and priceless.

'This is really something,' said George with admiration. 'I must write something about this. Perhaps a Greek newspaper will be interested in publishing it. I am sure that people in Greece are not aware that such things exist here.'

We agreed that if possible we would return and do a proper interview with Pasko the next day. After everyone was satisfied with the collection the smiling archaeologist, as always very happy to share the fruits of his labours with interested guests, showed us out and went back to his work.

'Does he always work so late?' asked George.

'I think quite often,' I said. 'And you remember the picture of him he showed us, wearing scuba gear?'

'Yes.'

'They are excavating a 4,000-year-old settlement that is now under water, not far from where we are staying. People used to live in houses on stilts over the lake in Neolithic times. He wants to reconstruct one of them and make a museum there.'

'Remarkable,' said George. 'Now ... shall we?'

'Of course.'

The dark flat streets of old Ohrid, under which Pasko had once told me a whole different ancient city probably lurked, were still not full of people out for the night; it was too early for the customs of a Mediterranean country such as this. We thus got a head start, and the bars eventually became loud and crowded and we probably drank too much, but this was a night for celebration. When it was very late we found the car, this time intact, and we had beaten the boy who was supposed to be there to collect money for parked cars, who had given up and gone to bed at a more reasonable hour than us.

Chapter 5

'When we want to swim in the sea, we go to Ohrid.'

That is what the little boys in Pustec on quiet Lake Prespa had told me. It had seemed so sweet and so hopeful then, but this morning Ohrid really had been transformed. The waves were huge and steely and crashing on Pestani, foaming as they slammed into the shore, sending spray over the red upturned hulls of the caïques on the beach. When the weather was like this on the lake you really could not imagine it could ever be any other way. We had wanted to go for a boat ride with Daniel's father but it was clearly not to be, at least not until the next day.

'Well then,' said George, 'what shall we do?'

We ate breakfast and thought it over and George

told my wife about how interesting the collection had been. 'Hopefully he will have time to see us again this evening before George leaves,' I said.

'Oh, so you decided!' said Buba. 'That's too bad! You should stay!'

'I would like to, but I must be back in Crete in a few days for the university.'

'That is,' I said, 'if the Leninists let you in.'

'Of course.'

We took the long, winding and forested high road to the far end of the lake, to Sveti Naum, the early 10th-century Byzantine church named for a saint who had performed and been associated with various miracles and oddities. You could still hear, it was said, the muffled thud of the saint's heartbeat if you put your ear to the cold stone coffin where he lay. The church was also home to peacocks and stood on a large cliff contemplating the sea (that is, the lake), and on its lawns and roof the birds pranced and cawed. In early summer, when their feathers were in full bloom, it was an unearthly show of colourful moving fans and unearthly cries and the occasional church bell marking time.

Sveti Naum was also where Marco's baptism had been the summer before. It was my idea and, despite the large volume of tourists who passed through it every day, we found that it was not difficult to arrange. For me, the idea of baptizing a baby in a church that was more than a thousand years old was highly appealing and it went off well, despite Marco shrieking when George handed him to the scary bearded man in black who dunked him in the cold water.

The most extraordinary part of it all, however, was how George – with some help from his mother, overseeing things from the side – was able to reply correctly in Greek to the priest, who was reciting the Orthodox liturgy for baptisms in Macedonian, a language he did not understand. But the rhythm and pace of it were similar enough that everyone knew where their part was and how to fill it, and this went on for long uninterrupted monologues as well, in streams of staccato church prayer.

When we reached the long sandy beach before the church we parked and walked across the bridge near where a sublime lake rested in the woods, reflecting light and trees like in a Japanese tea garden, and over the River Crn Drim, which rushed into the lake and left a wake of bubbles as it flowed out towards the center of it. Just a couple of days earlier we had been standing where the river came tumbling out of the lake, in Struga; here at the beginning it struck me how truly amazing this feat was, water going through water with so many chances to get lost in it, yet still holding together for over 30 kilometres until it reached the other side and continued on its way. It was just one of the many miracles of Lake Ohrid.

We walked up the hill and through the narrow arch in the high wall that enclosed the church. It was a revelation, with a red-tiled roof and pretty rounded domes, purely Byzantine, and beyond it, on the stone wall over the cliff, was the vast expanse of blue water far below and to the right Mount Galicica rising majestically into clouds running parallel down the wooded shore towards Ohrid.

'Marco! Look at the peacocks!' said my wife.

His little eyes bulged with excitement and he ran

off to chase the birds into rose bushes. The sun was coming out and the wind was less in this protected cove at the end of the lake. There was a huge well with a metal grate over the top into which people were dropping coins and making wishes or saying prayers, and Marco really enjoyed throwing the coins into the abyss.

Inside the church, it was dark until your eyes got used to it and the frescoes were very old and beautiful. Most of the surviving ones dated from the 16th and 17th centuries. The year before George had noticed various mistakes in the Greek orthography on some of them and concluded that they had not been created by a native speaker – probably by a Slavic monk who had been taught Greek later in life.

Indeed, the late 9th-century monk Naum, founder of the church, was an associate of St. Clement of Ohrid, who would establish the first 'university' in the Slavic world there. Indeed, while the monastery has variously been renewed and enlarged and suffered the usual fires over the ages, the church preserves early Cyrillic and Glagolitic inscriptions from as far back as the 10th century – making them among the oldest epigraphic evidence of Slavic literacy.

In 1806, the renowned Macedonian fresco painter Trpo came from Korche – probably over the same route we had to Pogradec, a couple of miles to the west – and then to the monastery, where he immortalized some of the miracles associated with Naum in art. *Harnessing the Bear* and *The Healing of the Mentally Disturbed*, for which Saint Naum was particularly known, were among them. Kleptomania was also commemorated in frescoes such as *The Stupefied Monk Who Tried to Steal the Body of Saint Naum from His Tomb*, not to mention *The Horse Thief Who Was Caught at the Gates of the Monastery Church at Dawn*.

The monk's tomb was sitting there in flat stone in one corner of the musty church and two little girls were waiting patiently to put their ear to the stone and listen for the saint's faint heartbeat. They giggled as they recognized it and sure enough Naum was still kicking, watching over his church.

We thought it a good idea to get to the beach while the weather was good. The beach near Sveti Naum was also one of the only sandy ones in Ohrid, and Marco loved playing with sand. It had been basically a week on the road and I had not been swimming since the ashen sea at Halkidiki when we were with the philosopher Frede. That seemed like hundreds of years ago now. I had been continuously thwarted by bulls, weeds and the weather, and was hopeful of getting a chance finally to swim. But then it started to rain and we had to pack up the plastic buckets and shovels and paddleball and retreat to the sleek hotel near the monastery for coffee. It had been part of the plan all along.

After that it was still raining and we decided to return to the house in Pestani, with a grumpy sleepless bear in the car. Everyone had a rest and we went out for a final dinner next door in the Desaret, where there was still, surprisingly, a strong representation of guests. The dining hall was cavernous and the floor clicked under women's shoes and it was draped in the kind of red upholstery and chair backs that could be forgiven for having seemed royal at some point in the recent past. There was a fixed menu of fish and salad and dessert and we ate, but quickly, as George wanted to see Pasko for an interview, before getting on the road back to Thessaloniki through Bitola and Florina in the dark. So he said his goodbyes to Buba and Marco, endowing the latter with godfatherly gifts and promised to see them again soon.

We went to Ohrid and found Pasko in Ohrid's best-known traditional restaurant, the Antico, decorated with Macedonian handicrafts and dark wooden beams and a roving troupe of musicians.

The affable archaeologist was happy to expound on the history behind the artefacts we had seen the night before and to explain his plans for excavations in the future to our Greek visitor. We were regaled with stories of the ancient tribes, the Enchelei and Desareti, Lychnidos, the city of light, the immortal remains of a sophisticated culture which had, in Pasko's estimation, hardly yet been discovered. 'There are over 4,000 known archaeological sites in Macedonia, and another 11,000 still to be looked at,' he said. As always, the problem was funds. 'But we hope we have secured enough to start work on the *Kiklopski Rid* (Cyclops

Hill) site, where I believe the lost city of Philip II to lie.' It was a prospect that filled him with immense delight. After our interview, George thanked the merry archaeologist profusely again for his time and for the replica ceremonial drinking cup he had been given at the museum.

'Boy! We really had an adventure,' said George, back at the Volkswagen. 'What stories I have to tell the people! Especially that Pustec ... that was really something.'

I wished George a safe trip and told him I would send the extra pictures. The camera he had bought in Israel while studying during the war six weeks earlier had little battery power left. And then he was gone in the darkness and I found a taxi man to take me back to the village and he said that there were more and more foreign tourists this summer but that those from Skopje were still as impolite as ever.

After George left things slowed down. It was a tectonic shift, like those that had pushed up mountains and created the lakes of Macedonia, and it took a few days to accustom myself to not visiting a different place every day at a controlled yet frenetic pace. The book tour had essentially become a family vacation but there were worse things than that. We had breakfasts on the outdoor balcony of the Desaret looking out over the well-groomed pines and the beach, with fried eggs or as they were described in Macedonian, *jajca na oko* ('egg on eye'), bacon and salad and cheese, except for my wife, who had a deep irrational fear of it.

'Do you realize I haven't gone swimming yet?' I said on the morning after George left. It was what I loved most and I hoped the weather would improve, or else I would just have to scare her by charging into the foam. I felt supremely protected in the water, in any case, but the lake in its whipped-up state did have the occasional floating branch to watch out for. But on the hotel beach, which had been enhanced by sand, the waterfront was open for a long stretch and when the sun peeked out I went in. It was cool but not cold and I enjoyed banging my head into the waves and diving over them very much. It was exhilarating and built up an appetite.

'Can Marco go swimming today?' I said, bobbing around back at the dock.

'Absolutely not. It is too cold.'

'But he has that protective layer of blubber, he won't feel a thing,' I argued.

She looked peeved. 'Maybe tomorrow.'

That settled it and I came out and helped fill buckets with sand and turn them over into tightly-packed sand-castles which he delighted in smashing with his small fist. If there was any baby more adorable than Marco, you could not have told it to us. With his plump cheeks and deep blue eyes and smiles that warmed you more than raki, he was simply the best. 'All parents *think* that their child is the best,' I said, 'but I *know* that he is the best.'

'Yes he is,' she said. 'But you should still not say so to every person we meet! I know you are proud of him but sometimes they might not understand.'

There was a tiny chapel, a new one, opposite the hotel at the top of the road going through Pestani. Marco enjoyed very much going there in the evening and kissing the saints – he called them all '*dedo*' ('grandpa') – who stood impassively in the icons. There were many grandpas to kiss and he also helped with lighting candles. He took instructions very seriously and clutched the small amber candle while someone lit it and then took it from his hand before the wax could drip and burn him. Then the candle was placed in the sand of the candle tray and he was satisfied.

'Why don't we try to take that boat ride today?' I said to my wife one morning. The weather had steadily been calming and the birds were chirping while we ate cereal on the breakfast table outside the house. Daniel's father was ambling around the garden doing his chores and we asked him about it. He thought that the weather would hold, if we set out soon enough. We prepared ourselves and jumped into the boat, a small blue-hulled caïque which was moored off of a long wooden dock on the right-hand side of the hotel beach.

Like other families in the Ohrid area, our host, now retired from a long career as a philology teacher, had a sideline in accommodating tourists and ferrying them around the lake in the summer. Now the season was ending and the engine was non-committal at first, but after some insistent tugging it sputtered to life and we were off, hugging the shoreline south to the hidden church of Sveti Zaum.

It was one of the most special places in Ohrid, hidden by trees at the base of a cliff, only accessible by water, near the most inscrutable part of the lake, around 1,000 feet deep. To get there we passed through green waters that looked almost tropical in the sun against white shores thick with lush trees. Behind all of it were cliffs, either direct and sudden or tapering behind, occasionally broken up by beaches. The biggest of them was Gradiste, popular for camping, near where Pasko Kuzman had discovered the submerged Neolithic settlement. There were other, more secluded coves, 'wild beaches', as our host called them. 'Daniel and his friends go camping there sometimes, where the caves are. Fishermen might pull into the caves when the weather is rough too.'

As if a reminder of Ohrid's temperamental moods, an old and half-sunken wooden hull lay stricken against a rock on the shore. Further out, near us, a grey rubber raft was filled with police divers. They were practicing flipping backwards into the water and this interested Marco very much. 'Mama! Look! Funny uncles swimming!' he sang. In Macedonian, to a child every man or women, depending on their relative age, was either an aunt or an uncle, a grandmother or grandfather. In a country of only two million, where familial ties were strong and people were generally friendly, it was not entirely without sense. Still, it was rather funny to hear everyone from the postman to a saint to a TV star referred to as 'grandpa'.

Then, around a corner, a landmark came into sight: the large jagged rock which I had used to measure distance while swimming the summer before. The rock was clustered with cormorants and we could pass very close to it because the water became very deep only a few feet from where it suddenly appeared. For some reason Daniel's father wanted a photo of himself driving the boat with the rock as a backdrop and I obliged. 'There is Trpejca now,' said my wife, 'Marco, do you remember Trpejca?'

Around the arc of the bay the village appeared, its neat tiled houses gathered on the beach of round stones and rising up the hill to where the Ohrid-Sveti Naum road passed by, and on the other side Mount Galicica overseeing all. They called it the 'Macedonian San Tropez', only half-jokingly, the least developed getaway on the coast, with a beach of rounded white stones that became manageable pebbles as you entered the azure water. We had stayed in the village for six weeks the summer before, and would always remember it for the traditional houses and friendly people, the mountain freshness and refreshing lack of organized civilization. Daytime meant regular coffee of various degrees of sweetness, green darting lizards and splashing in the clear water with an ebullient red-cheeked baby; night began with enormous sunsets and gave way to a resonating volley of frogs croaking from the unseen shore below.

For a few precious weeks, time did not exist. I would write in the mornings under a generously grape-laden trellis overlooking the water and swim in the afternoons. There was a billiard table in the old kids' recreation café, and no internet. There was fresh fish and meat in the small restaurant and the water was so clear that when there was sun – which was most of the time – green shafts of light penetrated down, down, down and disappeared. But when the clouds obscured the sun the water became black and it was like losing an old friend, even if it was one who had always been mysterious.

The man who rented us the house had been concerned lest the alleged cold springs cramp up my calves and I drown, which scared me at first though it soon became inconsequential. He was far less concerned about something which worried us tremendously, namely the scorpions that sporadically clung to a plastered wall somewhere. 'Ah, them,' he would laugh, squashing the menacing insects with his fist. 'They never hurt anyone.'

All saints have name days, feast days, which the Orthodox celebrate regularly and especially if a family member is named after the saint. There were was no one named Zaum, but sometimes you'd find someone named Naum, and there was an injunction against swimming on his feast day. It probably had less to do, I thought, with the fear of divine retribution than with the possibility that someone with a bellyful of roasted meat and alcohol had once drowned. Nevertheless, I did not dare to tempt his wrath.

The church at Sveti Zaum was dedicated to the Mother of God and had shown similar powers a few days earlier when, on the eve of the sacred day, a massive lightning storm surged right across from the Albanian side and through Trpejca, bringing with it roaring winds and agitated waves, heavy rain and even hail. The dirt path up from the lake through the houses was washed away and boats washed up on shore. When the storm sped on over Mount Galicica and on to the east, the air was clean and cool and silent, except for the surf pounding in long measured rollers into the beach. The sacred storm had washed the sky and the stars were so close they practically fell into your arms like fish.

I remembered all these things as we passed the village and its little fleet of caïques bobbing before it. 'Maybe we can stop there on the way back,' I said to my wife. 'We can eat lunch!' I thought about eating very often.

Just after the village, on the wild cliffs to the south, Daniel's father pointed out a recess in the cliff where a very faint fresco peeked out. 'An ancient hermit's dwelling,' he said. The tiny crevice was hardly out of keeping with similar inaccessible havens of asceticism throughout the Byzantine world. It was said that Ohrid, the once powerful archbishopric and Tsar Samuel's capital in the 10th century, in those days had had 365 churches, one for every day of the year.

The forested cliffs around the lake provided both a stunning setting for grand churches like Sveti Naum, and hidden places like this cliff cave. Centuries and centuries of spirituality had not failed to influence the lake, I thought, infusing it with divine insight; or perhaps the monks and hermits had just channelled the pre-existing wisdom of its fathomless depths. It was an uncertain, unsound thought and I suddenly jerked back from the bright sky and mountaintops playing out along the clear water surface. 'Hey! What are you doing! You will get us wet!' scolded my wife. I started rocking the boat, and then they did, and it was all fun until we were interrupted to look at the blood on the rocks above.

'Here they are!' said my wife, pointing to the jagged outcroppings pointing out of the cliffs and run through with bands of red mineral. Like with other natural apparitions, there were legends accounting for the rocks which the Ohrid people knew.

'What is the story behind this?'

'It is the frozen depiction of two brothers who could not agree on how to divide a goat,' said our host. 'And they beat each other bloody. When you view it from the mountain, it looks like one of them is falling down.'

I had heard a different legend, from another Ohrid local. 'A man told me that the rocks are the forms of two medieval princes who were killed after they kidnapped an Albanian princess from across the lake. Rather than be queen she killed them both with a knife in their sleep.'

'I don't know that one.'

'Well, the guy who told me was drunk most of the time,' I conceded.

It was destined to remain a mystery and soon we had reached the welcome curve of the shore guarded by a lone sloping tree behind which the church of Sveti Zaum – in full, the Sveti Bogorodica (Mother of God) Zuhumska – stood. It was set in the shade of the cliff, with distinctive Byzantine arched eaves and a central dome, burnt-red brickwork in the shapes of diamonds and long bars and mazelike patterns, all daubed by grey wattle in which green lizards hid.

The church was not usually open but this time it was. It was musty and it took time to get used to the darkness. Marco was very happy to kiss more grandpas and light more candles at the icons near the altar, the only new additions to a structure mottled with different layers of frescoes blended in a haze of incongruous colours.

'Look here,' said Daniel's father, pointing at one worn fresco. 'This is the only place where you can find Jesus and Mary depicted as king and queen.' I didn't know if it was true but I had certainly never seen such a thing before. An inscription stated that the church, and the frescoes, dated back to 1361. It was a humbling thought, to imagine that almost six-and-a-half centuries of storms, accidents, Turks and then Communists had not been able to dislodge Sveti Zaum. But seeing what he had been able to do with lightning the year before I was not completely surprised.

'There are two legends about the origins of this church,' said our guide. 'Both involve Saint Naum. The first states that he built his church originally here, but since it was far away from any road, no one could see it or get to it, and so he said to himself, "What was I thinking? With what mind did I do this?" This is because the word "zaum" comes from "za", meaning "for", and "um", meaning "mind". So we get the idea of for what mind or out of what thinking something was done'

'Interesting.'

'The second involves a rich noblewoman who was curious to know how deep was the deepest part of the lake. Saint Naum got angry because he had the key for the lake. He controlled the river Crn Drim and therefore however much water he would allow into the lake, that was how deep it would be. She said, "With what mind I was thinking to try and know the unfathomable?"'

For me, these odd legends illustrated perfectly the unique nature of Byzantine spirituality, itself patterned on the most ancient of the Church fathers and before them the Platonists, obsessed with the impossibility of absolute knowledge. Ohrid was as dramatic a place as any to prove this thesis. The primordial geology that expressed itself in the lake some three million years ago crushed up porous mountains, inviting division between one lake, Prespa, and the other, lower one, which became a vast, uneven chasm that gradually flattened out somewhere far from the shore. And so it was that the 1,000-foot mark of Ohrid, the lake's deepest point, was somehow only just past the church of Sveti Zaum, a couple of hundred yards off shore.

A ruined convent and blackberries awaited us outside the church, when we re-emerged from the musty darkness and Marco had stained his little hands purple busily eating the fruit of the vines that grew near the ruined second building of the church. 'The bear is getting hungry,' said my wife. 'Maybe we should go and eat something.'

We agreed and soon shoved off back for Trpejca. After ten minutes we reached it, pulling up at the dock on the far end of the village. We walked along the rocks of the beach to a restaurant we had frequented often the summer before, where the 17-year-old daughter of the family who had accommodated us worked; she was to be married to the son of the restaurant owner. She was very surprised to see us and, like George, remarked on how much Marco had grown. He dimly remembered the girl, another one of the ephemeral 'aunts' in his young life, and smiled showing all his baby teeth and asked for ketchup.

We ate quickly, as the weather was starting to change and Daniel's father, the veteran boatman, was becoming apprehensive about what the afternoon might bring on the lake. We left the little village with promises to come back when we could and set off in the small blue boat.

We had to go slowly because the waves were getting stirred up, and the blue sky was changing to grey. Yet the more that the caïque rolled, the more soothing it became for the baby, who soon fell fast asleep despite the occasional spray of breaking water on his cheek. My wife was startled and even I was a little nervous, not for myself but for them, though our guide seemed to think it was nothing out of the ordinary.

'How much longer?'

'Ah, 20 minutes.'

They *always* said it would be just 20 minutes. Staring impassively into the rolling lake, our skipper had to keep pointing away from the crest of the waves, to try to ride them off down the side, and the little boat was lurching up and down with spine-smashing slaps to its poor beaten hull, and the water in broad sheets across us. I had been in plenty of oceans and seas in my life, and these were sea conditions, albeit on a lake; but what made it worse was precisely the fact that this lake had its own currents and contours and breaks in the mountain where wind fed it, and so the waves could come from any direction. It was

154

hazardous enough. Nevertheless, Marco slumbered peacefully through it all and was kept dry and only started to vociferate loudly when what had been for him a rhythmic-enough ride ended, back at the pier in Pestani.

'Waaaaaaaahh!'

My wife tried to hush him but it was obvious. 'We woke him up at the wrong time in his sleep cycle.'

'How the hell did he sleep through that that?' I asked. 'A miracle!'

We trudged back up to the house with our grumpy miracle infant and rested. The evening approached and the weather softened so that anyone then looking at the lake would have thought we had made up the whole thing about a perilous voyage in an unsafe boat. We took a walk through Pestani, stopping on the beach to hurl more rocks in the lake – Marco's new favourite pastime – and returned for dinner to the Desaret where, for the first time, we were the only people in the big dining hall manned by attentive, older waiters and waitresses in their Communist-era vests and ties.

There is nothing like getting doused with cold water and adrenalin to revive the appetite and I had an old standby – *selsko meso*, or 'village meat' – pieces of pork and mushroom and onion in a brown sauce served in an earthenware pot. It was good of them for thinking of it too, because restaurants were not always prepared for such elaborate dishes, especially when they were part of hotels that were winding down for the season. 'These wrap-around red couches are pretty cool,' I remarked. 'Space age.'

'Stop! You will fall down!' scolded my wife, as Marco tried to stand up and jump on said red couches. He protested but sat down and looked with eagerness when they wheeled over a tray with the meat and cheeses and salad. 'Oooohh!' he said, and his eyes lit up. 'Food!'

Chapter 6

There is only one proper way to visit the major sites of mediaeval Ohrid when you are travelling with a small child who enjoys being carried, or with anyone who generally objects to walking uphill, and we had both. So, after taking the bus into Ohrid, we took a taxi for the brief journey to the gate in the enormous stone walls of the Tsar's castle, at the very top of the hill that gave Ohrid its name.

In the old Slavonic, and subsequently Macedonian, the word means 'on the hill', a reference to the high point where the mediaeval rulers built their fortress and guarded the wealth of the kingdom. Tsar Samuel, the proto-Bulgar ruler who also had his capital on the island of Saint Achilles in the Lesser Prespa Lake, left the fortress in Ohrid as a dramatic sign of his rule.

157

It was later used by the Ottomans when they took over.

It was a brilliant day, piercing blue skies everywhere and from the high walls of the castle you could see the rooftops of Ohrid below and the lake stretching out infinitely, placid and serene, through the sturdy parapets. My wife and I had to take turns to scale the fortress and walk around it because the stairs up were too steep and narrow for Marco. So he sat in the grass under guard, contentedly eating crisps and making up words. It was the latest favourite bit of mischief from a mischievous boy born in the year of the green wood monkey. 'Lanya, manya, tutska, futska,' he sang, breaking into roguish laughter when someone shouted '*Izmisluvas*!' ('You're making it up!').

Atop the castle a few tourists spread out along the ramparts, admiring the view from three sides, and in the center, where the Macedonian flag was rippled by the occasional breeze a lone man with a *gajda*, the lesser-known cousin of the Scottish bagpipes, was wailing out exotic Balkan strains for a few coins from the tourists. The music was droning and penetrated the sky all around and made me wonder if the sentinels in old times, or pipers heralding victory or perhaps a funeral – it was unearthly enough for any interpretation – had done the same in the same place.

From the castle we carried on down a tree-lined path and soon stumbled upon a wood-roofed enclosure to the left. 'What do you suppose that is?' I said. It turned out to be ruins, essentially just stone and mosaics, of a basilica that had been built sometime between the 4th and 6th centuries – the seminal period of early Byzantium, following Constantine the Great's decision in the year 322 to make Christianity, previously persecuted, the official religion of the eastern Roman Empire, now based in his new city of Constantinople on the Bosporus. Increasingly pious emperors, influenced by churchmen, went on to transform the New Rome into a bulwark of Christianity against pagan, and later Muslim invaders.

The basilica must have been a large one, and a beautiful one judging by its floor work. Roman flourishes were everywhere, in the peacocks and other birds, braided rings and what looked to be a reclining unicorn. 'Look, Marco, peacock,' I said, pointing down. His memory was astonishing. '*Kako vo crkva!*' ('Like in the church'), he said, remembering the peacocks of Sveti Naum. The mosaics showed that they had a long lineage indeed in the Ohrid area.

From the basilica we continued through a forest of well-spaced pines on a flat stone path down the hill to Plaosnik, its three domes in shadow and the lake for the first time emerging to the right below. It was a truly remarkable achievement, a basilica rebuilt in 2002 exactly to its Byzantine dimensions envisioned by its founder Saint Clement in the 10th century. Unsurprisingly enough, the project was led by our larger-than-life archaeologist friend Pasko, who had enlisted master stonemasons from the Macedonian villages of Prespa in Albania to create it. Spaced around it outside were squares of sand where lingered the remains of the earliest church, such as standing columns in the front of it and mosaics under glass. Previous layers of Plaosnik's life could also be seen inside the church, part of the ancient foundations illuminated under glass and fragments of frescoes fixed to the wall, cracked but in their proper places, like a puzzle on the verge of completion. The centrepiece of the church, however, was the tomb of Saint Clement.

Across from the church there were a few tables with vendors selling tee-shirts and jewellery and ice cream. 'Let's buy him one of these!' I said to my wife. It was a red shirt with the word 'Makedonija' printed across it and the 16-rayed sun of Vergina. With the floppy yellow hat and red shorts he already had, his blonde hair and red cheeks, adding the shirt made Marco look like a confused mix of ketchup and mustard.

'It's absolutely classic!' I said. 'I love it!'

'Marco and you should take a photo here,' said my wife. Indeed, it had to be done. We sat on the stone path in front of the church and fired off some shots. *'Marko e Makedonski vojnik?'* ('Is Marco a Macedonian soldier?'), she said. *'Da – Marko Makedonski vojnik!'* he cried out excitedly. He always enjoyed being the center of attention and with that uniform he was certain to be so today.

After Plaosnik the trail swept down and around

the corner, opening through the trees to the lake and before it the Byzantine Church of Sveti Jovan Caneo, its one dome outlined against the horizon, set on a crumpled star of brickwork, the simple, square convex base of the church. All of it lay in shadow except the curving red-tiled eaves which caught the sunlight dazzling the lake. From far above they looked like snakeskin, but when you came closer the tiles glinted evenly and plainly and it was impossible to imagine how many people had witnessed this stunning scene of the cliff church against the lake since it was built in the 11th century.

Caneo features in more photographs of Ohrid than perhaps any other place. Both the view from above, and then the view from being there, of the endless expanse of the lake and the town way down to the left, are matchless and remind one again that the Byzantine aesthetic sense, at a time when religion was the primary outlet for art, was most fulfilled in building churches or hermitages in places of great natural beauty, and in blending the structures with the terrain.

My wife relaxed on a bench in the shade of a fir tree overlooking the lake far below and I took Marco in through the narrow entrance of the church so he could kiss more grandpas and light more candles. The kindly old keeper of the church took a liking to Marco and gave him a candle for free, and I picked him up to light it and place it in the sand. His little heart was beating fast and his chest was heaving up and down with great breaths after so much walking. He wanted to make two tours around the little church, kissing icons, and I imagined that with his propensities he must be the most blessed little boy in all of Macedonia.

The lake surface was rippling slightly in the breeze and small boats occasionally passed across it. Now we had to go up before going down, and it was very hot. 'We can eat in that lovely fish restaurant and I will take a swim, okay?' I said.

'Yes, he missed his nap and he is probably very hungry.'

After a few minutes of walking up and down a hard path we came into the trees and finally emerged down at the water. To the right, crouched at the bottom of the dependable high rock upon which Caneo stood, was a tiny chapel opening onto the lake, while to the right red or blue-painted rowboats lay on the shore. We walked past them and onto a beach of white stones that crunched under your feet as you went, and bronzed sunbathers would look up warily from the towels upon which they lay. It was a splendidly sybaritic affair of lapping waters where people splashed and rocky outcrops where couples lounged and bikini-glad girls dipped delicate painted toes in the soft water.

Where the beach ended umbrellas stood on the patios of two café-restaurants. The second, the *Letna Bavca* ('Summer Garden'), was an Ohrid classic and a place I had always gone to for the *plasica* (small fried fish), the atmosphere and the proximity to the water that made swimming followed by lunch a definite option. It was all outdoors, facing the lake and bordered at the sides by bamboo rails, while the back of it was built into an old house that the restaurateurs' family had lived in for centuries. A walkway led into the lake and an overfed fluffy cat made the rounds of the tables, serenading guests with plaintive 'throw-me-some-fish' meowings.

'Oof! We are tired,' pronounced Buba. 'It is very hot.' The restaurant was packed with people, some suntanned and full and some just reading the paper and sipping coffee. Marco wanted water and the waitress came over with a smile and some menus. My wife ordered a coffee and said she would order the rest of the meal in ten minutes, which meant the fish would be ready in 30, and so I went off to swim.

At the Letna Bavca you got into the water from a small concrete dock just beyond the tables, and tried to avoid the rocks overgrown with aquatic life on the bottom and the buoys anchored by fishermen, which became less frequent and then disappeared the further out you got. I headed north-northwest in a big white plume of spray, the sun on my back in the warmth of a late summer Ohrid afternoon. Although most of the tourists had left by early September, in truth the water was actually at its warmest then; though the sunny weather began in May, the cold springs and snow runoff gave a false optimism at first. It took a few weeks for the lake to acclimatize itself to visitors but when it did it was wonderful.

After a few minutes I rounded the cliff and now everything was in a whole new perspective. I was at the same spot in the water which I had gazed down on from above the church of Caneo, scarcely an hour before. But now I was part of the lake, rather than part of the view, and in the water's warm caress I felt greater peace than I had through just that ephemeral sense, vision. There were nice rocks to swim close to and interesting currents and occasionally a small boat with tourists or a fisherman would pass by. I would wave to them or give some kicks to remind them I was there and eventually when I was satisfied I turned back towards the restaurant.

'That was great,' I said.

'I couldn't see you! You know I hate it when I can't see you!'

'Come on,' I retorted. 'You know about my divine protection in the water – and in front of a church, too! Will the food come soon?'

'I hope so. You should do something about your son. He is getting bored with waiting.'

'Aha!' I said. 'Time for throwing rocks!'

I took Marco down to the beach of white stones and he sat there next to me with his yellow sun hat and red-and-yellow tee-shirt on. '*Silno!*' (Powerfully!') he intoned, hurling stones into the water where they fell with an apologetic pop or a bigger splash when he got it right. It was a very serious business for him. When my wife signalled that the food was ready he didn't want to give up throwing rocks, and it was only the sight of the food that stopped his tears of protest. '*Ubovo!*' ('Beautiful') he said.

We had forgotten how big the portions were and had ordered two plates of *plasica* whereas one would have done just fine. Together with the salads and crunchy bread and beer, it was a real meal. The little fish were cooked whole and some people ate them that way, but you could see the outline of the eyes and very tiny teeth and so I didn't. They were a little charred but very golden and delicious and accompanied the beer perfectly. My wife was only distressed when one, and then more of the bulging *plasica* were found to contain small eggs. 'This means we are eating pregnant fish,' I said.

'Oh! That's very sad,' she said. 'But they are very tasty!'

We enjoyed the lunch, myself most of all after the exhilarating swim. The afternoon was coming to its peak, when dogs slept but cats evidently still foraged for fish, and Marco became very animated every time he saw the cat or it brushed against his leg under the table. There was far too much fish for us to finish, and the cat ended up happy indeed.

After the lunch we felt sleepy but vowed to defer coffee as a sort of reward for making it down again to the entrance of the old town. There was a narrow cobbled road that covered the distance, passing by the stately traditional homes of the old families of Ohrid, with tiled roofs at sloping angles to one another, all overlooking the lake, undulating red balanced on outspreading blue. 'Wouldn't it be nice to live here?' said my wife. 'It certainly would,' I answered. 'Look, Marco, a cat!'

He ran to chase the cat and we got to a point where the road forked and led down long steps to the alleys of the old town. The most prominent structure at the bottom was another church, the grand Sveti Sofia, a long, rectangular church with an arched roof and one tiled dome, and round pillars running around the outside. It had been built in the 11th century and ever since had been known for its acoustics, being used during the Ohrid Summer Festival in July, and at other times when a cultural 'manifestation' (as Macedonians amusingly termed such events), was to take place. Two years earlier, when I had been to a concert by the famous Macedonian opera singer Boris Trajanov in those Byzantine confines, I could imagine how, in medieval times, the pyrotechnics and incense and music of the Byzantine liturgy would have trans-fixed the congregations inside.

As we entered the old town it became busier, with people out for a summer stroll under the archways in the narrow stone streets. The houses were either multi-angular and white with brown shutters, in the old Ohrid style, or built of stone, sometimes coloured, sometimes not, set on paved lanes linked by winding stairs or narrow passages.

We reached the end of it along the bottom route, with the old tiled houses at unruly angles rising to the top of the hill, where the walls of Tsar Samuel's castle looked down on everything. We were on the square, flanked by cafés and facing the water, near to the great stern statue of Saints Cyril and Methodius, the Byzantine monks from Thessaloniki whose missions to the Slavs of the Balkans and Central Europe changed the course of history, introducing a form of writing and a religion, and thus a civilizing influence, to the previously pagan tribes of the region.

All the cafés were strung together and all were more or less the same, so we sat down at an empty table and ordered iced coffee for us and plain ice cream for Marco. The others were getting tired but there was still a possibility for me to get an interview with the oldest living woodcarver in Ohrid, and this was something I did not want to miss. So after we had enjoyed some caffeinated sweetness and the Ohrid ethos, my wife and son returned to Pestani and I went with Mitko, a young Ohrid woodcarver, to visit his workshop and his 87-year-old grandfather Dimitrije in their spacious home in the old town.

I was warmly greeted by the family and given small sweets. On the walls samples of the maestro's work – icons and intricate flower-motif carvings hewn from walnut or cherry wood. We sat on couches and the old man told of his life of woodcarving in the lakes. He had a wave of white hair and weathered skin and was a little hard of hearing, yet still took pride in telling his story and soon warmed to the occasion.

'I am from the generation of the night school,' said Dimitrije, 'when the Serbian king Alexander Karadjordjevic decided to fund the renaissance of wood carving in Ohrid.' The Serbians who took control of the upper half of Macedonia in 1913 had been impressed by the devilishly intricate and massive iconostasis at Sveti Jovan Bigorski Monastery in Debar, north of Ohrid, and they wanted to bring the tradition back to its former greatness. Woodcarving was important in the Macedonian religious tradition, just as the Armenians were known for stonework, the

171

Italians for painting or the French for stained glass. It was part of the national heritage of a people born of the forests, lakes and streams of a rugged country rich in timber.

'In 1926, there were only six students left in Debar, so they decided to move the school to Ohrid,' said the old man. 'The students were generally farmers, who worked the fields in the day and studied at night. At first, the school was divided between those who wanted to be carpenters and those who wanted to be carvers. In my generation, there were thirteen carvers, but only four became good. They are not alive anymore.'

'How did it go, the classes?'

'First they put us in the old churches,' he said. 'We had to draw the motifs of the carvings there – you can't start anything without the drawings – and then for two years we were moulding them in clay. Then we began with the wood.'

'Why did you choose this profession?' I said

He laughed. 'My father was a farmer and I had six brothers and sisters. My father couldn't afford to send us all to school. I didn't want to be a farmer too. So I learned to love woodcarving.'

From the way Dimitrije reverentially pointed to his sculpted examples on the wall, and led us through a photo album of his other works, it was clear that he did. He had vivid stories of the Italian, then the Bulgarian occupation of Ohrid during World War II, when he was with Tito's Partisans but was captured and, inexplicably, released in Serbia. Like so many others of his generation, the war sent Dimitrije on a far-flung route through the Balkans; he sold his artwork in Plovdiv, in south-central Bulgaria, and continued on to Varna on the distant north-eastern Black Sea coast where his brother was working as a shipwright. Dimitrije also found work in the boatyard, but came home after the war and returned to carving and the school, now run by one of Tito's men.

'So, we weren't doing church decoration anymore,' he said.

Indeed, the political change simultaneously turned the talents of the carvers away from the ecclesiastical, but the impressiveness of the finished result remained the same. Dimitrije was soon crafting ornate walnut desks, cabinets and chairs for the office of Tito himself. The great leader was so pleased, in fact, that he came all the way from Belgrade to see the wood-carvers of Ohrid in action.

'He always tells this story,' whispered Mitko, leafing through the photo album to where a newspaper clipping from 1957 had been carefully inserted. 'He's very proud of it.' The article quoted the Yugoslav leader thus: *I think that this art is of great importance for our country and I'm very satisfied that I have had the opportunity to see in person this creativity from the workers in Ohrid.*

'What was it like?' I asked. 'Were you nervous?'

'Oh, I was very nervous,' said the old man. 'After all, this was the leader of Yugoslavia standing right in front of me and my work! It was after we had made him a very nice gift for his office.'

'Was he pleased with his visit?'

'Tito was overcome with emotion, and he didn't know what to say,' recalled Dimitrije proudly. 'The person in charge of his schedule said, "Okay, time to move along" after 20 minutes, but he said, "No, let me stay a little longer to look at this great art." I was very happy.'

Nevertheless, the school closed in 1962 and it was left for the individual carvers to preserve the tradition by handing it down to descendents – as Dimitrije did with his 33-year-old grandson who, together with his fiancée, worked in a narrow workshop in the very top of the house under the old man's tutelage. The room had two long tables on which large blocks of wood rested under strong lamps and a range of vises and hammers and chisels were arrayed near them. I watched them chip away little angles out of the wood, in line with pencilled-in contours, bringing it to life with the outlines of flowers and vines and animals and saints.

'So, are these the same kind of tools as those used by the Debar school craftsmen in the 19th century?' I asked.

'Well, this is the biggest mystery,' said Mitko. 'Similar, but it's still a mystery as to what exactly they used to achieve that incredible three-dimensionality and precise detail. After they finished the iconostasis at Sveti Bigorski, the story goes, the carvers' tools were thrown into the River Radika so that no one could replicate the great work of art.'

'Amazing. Do you always use a certain kind of wood?'

'Yes, we use walnut. Macedonia is very rich in trees, there is no need to import them.'

'We go in the Ohrid and Prespa-area villages,' said the old man, 'and the people know us. They'll say, "Hey, Dimce, I have a nice big walnut tree. You want to buy it? Or else I will use it for kindling." Many people don't know the value of a walnut tree.'

'Then we store them to dry,' said Mitko. 'At least one year, depending on the thickness. Now there are machines to mechanically dry the wood in only twenty days, but the result is inferior. Naturally-dried wood is better to work with.'

They told me that despite its long heritage and cultural value, woodcarving would be endangered unless the government gave funds to formalize education and subsidize projects.

'So if they did, is it possible that you could do work equal to the classical age of the Debar School?'

'Everything is possible,' said Mitko. 'Like any other job, it just depends on how much time you can afford to spend on it. To make more and more intricate details means we have to spend a lot more time on it.'

No one was optimistic that the government would come to the rescue of wood-carving – it was just one of the many social and cultural programs competing for state attention, and hardly the most vociferous – Dimitrije, Mitko and his fiancée were all happy with their family tradition and success. The big pieces on the table being worked on at the moment, I learned, were destined to become the iconostasis in a Macedonian diaspora church in Australia.

Dusk was now approaching and so I thanked the oldest living woodcarver in Ohrid and his family very much for their hospitality and time, and ventured out into the street where birds were chirping aimlessly from the eaves and the evening sky over town and lake had turned a soft burgundy. Many people in summer clothes were out for an evening stroll on the long, wide pedestrian street that led up from the square to where an enormous plane tree several hundred years old stood indifferently in the midst of it all. The first lights were coming on in the shops and there was music in the cafés. Something inside of me took note of it, in passing, as I left that world and went to find a car that would take me to the village of Pestani.

Chapter 7

A cloud of purple spread in the shallow water where the women were washing blankets, on a coast well past the village covered in white stones. It was doubtless an age-old tradition and they said they did it once a year. I had swum from Pestani, from the Hotel Desaret where my wife and son were playing on the sand in the sunshine, around many headlands and cliffs and now to the people washing blankets. Further on, a fisherman was sorting through his nets besides an old battered skiff.

The weather was getting better and better after the somewhat inauspicious beginning to our trip in Ohrid. I enjoyed nothing as much as than swimming in the lake, which was something I had not expected way back in the beginning since, having grown up on an ill-tempered, snapping-turtle-infested pond in central Massachusetts, I had been prejudiced against fresh water from an early age. Yet Ohrid was different. The lake was so vast, and the weather could be so fierce, that I thought the little boys of Pustec could be forgiven for thinking it was a sea.

The thinness of the water was always what struck me most about it. When the lake was quiet, it was almost as if it did not exist at all, so effortlessly and smoothly did it roll off your back. And there was no thick lake smell, no mosquitoes and not many weeds. Ohrid had the capacity to soothe you, but also to unnerve you; when the sun hid behind a cloud and those deep emerald rays went black, it was almost like a trap had been sprung and you were in the grip of the lake. But the sun always came out again.

Like areas of land, all bodies of water have spirits and, as I shoved off again to trace the contour of the coast, I wondered what Ohrid's was and how it manifested itself. The water was cool and had a very faint fresh smell and was very clear. You could not see the bottom but you could see wonderful bubbles of different sizes and intensities when you pushed the water with your hand. Certainly the water and the many churches and monasteries built along Ohrid's banks had been in some eternal communion, some synergy of purpose and mind that expressed itself in the writings of the Eastern Church, at the same time simple and lucid and enigmatic. *This is not a Roman Catholic lake*, I thought. *It is too refined and ethereal for that.*

It was also a lake without an island, something that struck me as odd considering its size. Even the Lesser Lake Prespa had a relatively large one, Agios Achilleos. So how could Ohrid not have one? It was an insoluble problem but I concluded that a detached piece of land emerging from those unfathomable depths would have merely interrupted the concentration and taken away from the unity of Ohrid's being. There was no fixed point in the water for sailors to navigate by; there was no stopping *en route* to one place or another. It was what made the other shore look so deceptively close, though it was between 11 and 13 kilometres away. The middle of the lake was a place where no one had any business being, something that could be crossed only at the risk of one's life, or at best very slowly, though divine messengers such as lightning could be superconducted across it in seconds.

I floated on my back in the sun and listened to the water. It transmitted many things, like the muffled roar of a motorboat from far away or the sound of the water itself in your ear which was like a creaking door, or the modest splash of a frog from a rock or a bird skimming the surface for fish. And sometimes, if you were still, a fish would even jump out of the lake of its own accord. But you had to keep your legs going because the water was very light and very indifferent.

This was perhaps what was most frightening about the lake, understood strictly in a spiritual sense, for there was nothing – neither fish nor snakes nor turtles nor anything else – that could harm you physically. But when you swam enough there you could communicate with those deep shafts of jade that dropped from the sun down into the endless depths, if you were willing to accept silence for a reply, and I understood that Ohrid was a body of water supremely indifferent to anyone's fate. It would not inhibit your free will, yet neither would it save you from yourself nor from anything else. It was above that. Ohrid was essentially liberated from this world and that is why so many ascetics and monks had gravitated to its shores in the first place. And it always gave you something back for what you put in but you had to put something in first.

I had now been out for a good hour or more and I was ready to go back to the hotel. I followed the coast once again, and this time came in closer to where I could see the large rocks underwater as I passed over them. It was of course warmer there, where it was shallower, and I luxuriated in the water, only reluctantly forcing myself to get out.

'*Tata*!' said Marco, greeting me excitedly.

'I will take him swimming quickly, okay?'

'Is it cold?' my wife said.

'No, it is fine. I feel very good.'

I went to the side of the beach where there were

big flat stones and I sat down in them with Marco sitting in front of me. He was slapping the water and kicking it furiously and yelling *'Silno! Silno!'* to signal his intensity. We continued for 20 minutes or so and as usual he was crying at the end because he wanted to stay in. 'Tomorrow, Marco, you will swim more,' pleaded my wife.

'Marco! Be a good boy! Tomorrow you will swim in a *drugo ezero*! (a different lake),' I said.

We had decided to leave Ohrid the next day for the final leg of the trip, back to the lake I had glimpsed from its southern shores in Albania and Greece – Prespa. To get there we had to go back to Ohrid and then find a bus to Resen, a small town and *de facto* capital of the Prespa region. And so, after a final dinner in the flowery outdoor restaurant where we had gone the first night, we got our things ready and in the morning thanked our host and went to Ohrid.

There were only a few bags, and half of the things were children's toys. Still, it was hot and we did not know how long it would take to get to the far end of the lake, near the Greek border, which according to my unerring logistical sense would be the wisest thing to do. It would be better to get there sooner rather than later.

'Let's ask this guy,' said my wife, pointing to a man by a minivan. We were at the bus station but very often you could find a minivan or car driven by private taxi-men that would go faster and more frequently to where you want to go, and for more-or-less the same price.

'He's going to Bitola,' she said, coming back. 'Resen is on the way. Come on!'

We loaded the bags into the back of the van and had to wait a few minutes until another passenger could be found. But then we were off down a twisting road that passed through lush green forests and hills, only levelling off when we reached the outskirts of Resen. It was a small dusty town foreshadowed by orchards and populated with tractors and fading houses. Resen was famous throughout Macedonia for its apples, and though not directly on the lake itself but somewhat to the north of it, it was the gateway to the whole Prespa lake region, the principal town which had figured prominently in modern history, in the Macedonian revolutionary uprising of Ilinden in 1903, as well as the Young Turks rebellion five years later.

The man left us off near the bus station in Resen, which was as small and unobtrusive as the town itself. 'First let us get him some food,' said my wife. 'And me!' I added. We found one restaurant not far away that was as lavish as it was empty, and we ordered fish. Afterwards the waiter brought us special bowls of water with lemon and black pellets and bay leaves for washing our hands. Then, as in Turkey, a waiter broke out a dustbuster and started vacuuming up the crumbs on the table with it, much to the fascination of young Marco.

We were lucky, because it turned out that a bus for Dolno Dupeni, the most distant Prespa village, two kilometres from Greece, was about to leave. Although my wife had a distant relative in Resen, the far reaches of the lake represented a place neither of us had ever been. Truth be told, it was not in fact the end of the lake, just the point where the border with Greece began. But it was a wild, wooded border and, though there was a road, the crossing was closed.

The bus came and we left the dusty little station, and in a few minutes the lake came into view. There were tall reeds and plants and no major hotels or structures as in Ohrid, but rather a collection of small villages, few and far between. 'Look Marco,' I said, pointing at the water, 'here is your new lake!'

'Oooh!' his eyes lit up. '*Ezero!*'

After 30 minutes or so we left the lake at the old village of Nakolec and headed inland through the forests to Ljubojno and Brajcino, our penultimate stop before Dolno Dupeni. A Swiss foundation had helped Brajcino be reborn as an eco-tourism center where foreign tourists could stay in restored traditional houses and watch the locals prepare traditional meals for them. It seemed vaguely exploitative, until I heard the prices and realized who was being exploited.

'But you can find those kind of things in any village,' I protested.

'I don't know, maybe they do something special there,' said my wife. 'And even it's more expensive than some places, still you know it's nothing to Western tourists.'

'I know, but I'd rather stay in Dolno Dupeni. This is too far from the lake.'

'All right, but where will we find to stay there? Hello! The season is over!'

'Don't worry,' I said, 'we will find somewhere.'

The bus returned to the coast road and finally veered up into the village. It had a dependable cleanliness to it, as if it had been recently swept, and was made up of traditional stone cottages. 'Lovely,' I said. 'Will this woman help us?' asked my wife, pointing to a fellow passenger from the bus who had said she knew of private accommodation in the village. I went with her up a hill and into one house, but they had closed their doors to guests for the season. I returned to explain this to my wife, who was standing under a tree in the shade. She was tired and Marco was too, though he had slept fitfully on the bus, and I told her to wait there. 'I will find something,' I said. 'This

188

village has at least three streets and many houses. There has to be someone.'

I went up the opposite street, which seemed to lead towards what might pass for a center, though no one was on the streets. I walked by a small shop that was selling provisions and had, I noted, a billiard table, of all things, out front. There were some older men sipping beer on the patio of the shop and this was a good sign.

Then, where the road turned to go down, there emerged above on the right a long dirt driveway which ended in a flat place where some people were sitting in the shade under a tree. There were men in uniform, and young women, and as I got closer I saw they were Macedonian border police. They were sitting on upturned orange beer crates, and the women sat on a couch also supported by beer crates.

'*Dobar den* ('Good day'),' I began, but before too long one of the women brashly spoke in English. 'You are from America? You need a room? Okay, okay, I will help you.' She was slim, with dark hair and dark eyes and could almost have been Spanish, and spoke with the rounded, almost guttural accent of the Skopje native. 'I am Jelena,' she said, offering her hand. 'I think there is a hotel here. My grandmother knows. I will take you.'

'Wait,' I said, 'my wife is waiting to hear if I found something. I will be back.'

I went and explained to Buba what the situation was and picked up the bags. We came up the dirt driveway and greeted the people. Marco was very happy to see small children, a boy of about six and a slightly younger girl. They liked one another and soon were playing with a football I had been lugging around. 'They are my children,' said Jelena. Her husband was in Skopje and she was with them for a two-week vacation in Dolno Dupeni, her grandparents' home village. 'It is a very beautiful village you have here,' I offered.

'Yes. I know,' said Jelena. '*Ajde* (come on), let's try and get the key.'

I followed her down the hill and through the houses, where she waved at a thin old man clutching a very long sickle who looked like a living scarecrow when he waved back. It turned out she was an unemployed actress whose husband was a famous photographer. They had lived in Spain and, as I had guessed, she was part Serbian. I wasn't sure whether it was that fact or her profession that was to blame for her expressiveness.

"Hey! Grandpa! Where have you been?' said, Jelena, hugging an old man who was probably not related to her in the yard of an old house. She explained the situation and he nodded and sent us down a dirt track to a two-storey house with a gate outside. A middle-aged couple who lived nearby were the owners.

It was the village hotel, meaning the upper floor, with several rooms off a common hallway and a large concrete balcony with views of the lake outside. The room was small but good enough and there was no one else staying there.

'So you will take it?' she asked.

'Yes, it is fine.'

'How many nights?'

'Two,' I replied. It was better than saying one.

Despite the generally poor economic situation, I had witnessed plenty of occasions in which people, especially in Ohrid, would simply not open their doors to a guest staying only one night. 'For 1,800 denars, it's not even worth it to change the sheets,' one hotelier on the shores of Trpejca had announced haughtily when I had been looking for rooms the previous summer, for Neni and George and his mother. It was the equivalent of 30 euros and considering that that was basically 15 per cent of the average monthly salary, I thought it was damn well enough to change the sheets. But they saw things differently.

We walked back up the hill, successful, and Jelena was talking excitedly about all the things she could show us in the village. I had mentioned I was writing this book and was keen to talk to the people and get a sense of them and their experiences. 'I know the perfect guy for you,' she said. 'How close are we to the beach?' I asked. 'I would like to swim very much.' She pointed towards where the coast road was. 'Two kilometres down is a very nice beach.' 'Yes! We will go swimming.'

192

We went back up the gouged-out dirt driveway where Marco was playing with the kids and my wife was sitting with the others. 'We found a place,' I said. 'I think it will be okay. There's only us.'

'Good,' said my wife. 'I think he should take a nap.'

'Who is for coffee?' said Jelena. 'Come, I will show you my grandmother!'

We went down the stair behind the trees where her grandmother and a companion were sitting in full country bonnets stringing bright red peppers that would dry with the other ones that were already hanging from the eaves. One of them had socks and the other didn't, but I do not remember which.

They greeted us cheerfully and welcomed us to their village. Like many Macedonian village homes, the kitchen was recreated outside – from an old oven with a stove pipe and a great basin with running water and table and chairs, everything was there except for a refrigerator. It was because they did so much cooking and stewing and drying and baking that a large area was needed and you could hardly keep up with everything that was going on. The table was placed under a trellis of grapes but you could move it as the shade moved throughout the day.

We had good Turkish coffee and talked with the border police, stout young fellows in dark green uniforms, who spent their days beyond the beach and the indentation where the mediaeval Macedonian King Marko allegedly once set foot, overseeing the border with Greece. 'Ever any action there?' I inquired. 'Smugglers? Terrorists?'

'No, everything's peaceful,' they said. 'Nothing going on.'

'But you can't drive from here to Greece?'

'No, the border's been closed since ... what ... 1965?'

'About that.'

'Hmm,' I said, 'Do they have plans to open it?' I remembered taking the long route through Albania to get to this point, though it wasn't the only way.

'They say so,' said one of the policemen, 'but in a couple of years.'

'I talked to some people in Psarades, that is, Nivici

and the other villages ... some of them have relatives in Dolno Dupeni, they said.'

'Yes,' said Jelena, 'many people are related in this whole area.'

I thought about it. On the one hand it would be good to facilitate freedom of movement, especially for those who were all but cut off from their relatives. It was notoriously difficult for Macedonians to get visas for Greece, especially for the older ones who had been expelled from Greece during the Civil War. If your Yugoslav passport gave your place of birth in its original, Macedonian name, rather than the Helleni-cised one, there was no chance you would get a visa. The Greeks would coldly inform you that no such village existed.

I thought it likely that the Greek government did not feel the need to recognize the Macedonian minority because it was confident that it would die out soon enough, as most of them were old and the rest had long been assimilated. A diaspora activist from Canada had told me a few months earlier about a little girl in a village in northern Greece who was chastised by her grandmother for speaking in Macedonian. 'Hush!' said the old woman, who had lived through unspeakable repression. 'They will hear you!' Things were now quiet, but the Greeks still had their spies and collaborators, or so the beleaguered Macedonians thought. But they also had their European Union passports and standards which applied to most things except recognition of minorities. But a few thousand Macedonians were no danger to Greece.

Nevertheless, the whole tri-border lakes area was part of a grand European scheme led by the Eurocrats and non-governmental organizations obsessed with integration and creating multi-ethnic harmony, as concepts that would shore up Enlightenment values and their funding as well. Roads and new border crossings were just part of the programme of the Continent's new totalitarian freedom.

Perhaps selfishly, I imagined that opening the border road that had been closed since Yugoslav times would simultaneously destroy Dolno Dupeni's wildness, its sense of finality, of being the end in the way Borges had intended in his favourite story *The*

South, rather than just another village in a line of villages running along the lake. In other words, the border should exist for my pleasure. For better or for worse, for now it was that way and this made the moment all the more ideal for me, in the sense that it had been inferred in the story, if you looked at it from a certain way, that I was convinced rather vainly that only I had.

'*So Skopsko, ce e mozno*' ('With Skopsko, everything is possible'), the old beer advert had read, and indeed to me Macedonia had always been that country where indeed everything was possible. The finality of the border and the austerity of the village with a modest asphalt road and reed-beds near it only accentuated that ideal. It seemed the sort of place where providence or fate would indeed toss you whatever you needed to kill or be killed or avoid being killed, and there was no fog anywhere. Dolno Dupeni could be terminal but this time it was not.

After our coffee and conversation with the policemen we retraced our path. This time I was bringing up the rear with the bags, and Buba was talking with our new friend and Marco was dutifully plodding along with them. We reached the hotel and got the key just as the sun was setting. It was really a very beautiful view from the balcony and I was very glad that we had found this place. 'Now you will meet us tonight in the restaurant for dinner,' said Jelena. 'It is down this road to the main one, and then you go right 500 meters and it is on the left. I will see to it that they prepare a very good meal for us. *Ajde*, bye!'

We went in and put down our things and my wife sank down on the bed. It was too late for naptime, at least for Marco, and I took him back up to the center of the village where the bus had stopped, near a small school, and we played basketball on the simple half-court there until after it got dark. He really enjoyed being picked up in the air and throwing the football up. Even though it only went a few inches, he was proud of himself and we celebrated as if he had made every shot.

We came back and my wife was awake and we got ready to go. 'I will eat the whole restaurant,' I said. 'I hope it is good.'

We walked along down the road which was dark but the way was illuminated by a moon that was full or nearly so, in a sky bereft of clouds teeming with well-spread stars. The air was cooler than in Ohrid, as the elevation was slightly higher, and the breeze came in gently from the lake. It was silent except for the crickets and no cars passed us as there was nowhere for them to go.

The restaurant was down a stairway on the lake side of the road and reminded me of other old eateries I had found in the western mountains of Macedonia, cavernous and with long heavy tables and men in light jackets and sweaters drinking pints of beer. Jelena was already there, with her two children. She had taken matters into her own hands and prearranged a menu. 'They are winding down for the season,' she had said, 'but I will arrange that they will prepare a special meal for you.' She seemed confident of her powers and hospitable and I attributed this to a desire to show that she was someone in her ancestral village, despite that she only visited it once a year.

The dinner was truly larger than life, plates of ribs

and whole cooked fish and large salads and the *nafura* grilled bread with cheese that I liked so much. Marco liked playing with the cheese and eating tomatoes and meat. It was all very tasty and I resolved to eat slowly as then I could eat more. Anyway we had plenty of time.

Jelena started talking to my wife and though the chef was playing Macedonian music as robustly as he cooked, we could hear each other. She told us about the television show she had hosted in Skopje when she was pregnant for the second time, all about pregnancies and what you should do during them, both for men and for women. The final episode concluded with Jelena giving birth on television.

'My husband was the cameramen,' she said proudly. 'It was great – nobody in Macedonia could imagine something like that!'

Indeed, it was certainly flamboyant and the whole idea seemed like something they would do on American television. She told my wife sordid tales of the things that happened behind the scenes in the acting world, what the famous people and personalities of Macedonia did, and who they did it with, and how the whole scene was hypocritical and everyone pretended as if nothing was going on.

If she did not land a role in some new production, Jelena hoped to make documentaries about Macedonia's hidden villages, and she said this would be interesting for a famous foreign journalist like myself.

'But why don't you have a car?' she said. 'Wouldn't it make it easier for you to get to these places?'

'Oh you know, Skopje is small enough you don't need a car,' I demurred. 'Anyway, my licence expired years ago.' I didn't want to say that we were too poor for things like cars and she did not work it out either. By now the table was a veritable demolition site of gutted carp carcasses and mauled ribs, spent slices of lemon dotting the edges and tomatoes in oil. It was bizarre for me how, just a few kilometres away on the other side of the border, they would be using olive oil instead of vegetable oil and the carp would be served in golden fillets, rather than the whole fish cooked with its skin on.

After a while Marco grew restless and I took him

outside to play in front of the restaurant with the other children. There were apple trees there and one of the men from the restaurant came out and jumped up one of the trees to toss down some apples. 'Say thank you, Marco.' 'Ta-ank yooou,' he dutifully replied.

We went back in after some running around and Jelena was still talking to my wife about how she could help her in Skopje. 'What is the plan for tomorrow?' I said. She told me to come early in the morning, and we would go together to meet the old man of the village with a 500-year-old tree in his yard and many stories to tell.

'What about the beach? Is it far?'

'The entrance is two kilometres, it is too far to walk,' she said. She did not have a car, her husband had it in Skopje. I was surprised to hear that she had come on the bus like us.

'If we can get a lift we will go,' she said. 'Now be there early!'

We went back to our room where the outside light was on and many moths and mysterious lake bugs were congregating on the white plaster wall. I had eaten so much that it was hard even to lie down. 'You just need some exercise,' said my wife. 'You can swim tomorrow.'

'Even if we can't drive there, we can walk, right?'

'We will see how the day goes. I want to sleep in tomorrow morning.'

We pushed both beds together and slept and even Marco did not wake up in the night so often. In the morning I got up and left them, still sleeping, and went back to the house of our local leader. She was bright-eyed and ready to go and we marched down to the house of Dedo Spas, an amiable 72-year-old. He greeted us warmly, as did his wife. It was nine o'clock and starting to be a very hot day but we sat in the shade on his porch and drank Turkish coffee.

'There are many legends about the name of this village,' said the old man. I was already aware of the more vulgar; the word *dolno* means 'lower' and the word *Dupeni* that is a passive tense of a word, *dupenje* that means, essentially, 'drilling'. The village thus literally meant 'Lower Drilling', or, 'Those Being

Drilled from Below'. There were jokes on television programs and people did get a rise out of it.

Yet there were other stories. 'In 1018, Tsar Samuel saw his army, defeated by Byzantine Emperor Basil II at Mount Belasica,' said the old man. 'Besides being blinded, they had cuts and what looked like "drillings" in the lower parts of their bodies. It was near here, on the way to his palace on the island of Sveti Achil.'

'What others are there?'

Dedo Spas thought for a moment. 'There was a village, some 30 kilometres away from here, now in Greece, between Prespa and Kostur [Kastoria, in Greek], called Zhelovo. Somehow the people got angry with each other and couldn't live together anymore. So an archaic meaning of "Dupeni" was "fucking with your head". After enough of that the two tribes of the village left to form new villages – Dolno Dupeni and Gorno Dupeni, up near Resen.'

It was a mystery, but an amusing one. The old man told us stories more rooted in fact about his father, who had been born in 1896, and his grandfather, who had lived until 1920. 'My great-grandfather was born in 1850,' he said, 'but he never came down from the mountain.' In those times several villages that eventually moved to their present locations by the lake were on higher ground for fear of the Turks. 'There was a tower in the center of this village,' said Dedo Spas, as we continued on past his house and down the street to where the ruins of the house he was born in and the school that had only four grades stood. 'The important Turks lived there.'

'So, how many people live here now?' I said. There were few people to be seen, though there were many houses.

'About 300 live here full-time,' he said. 'But others keep summer houses, people who moved to Skopje or who emigrated to other countries. Now let's find that bandit Alekso.'

Dedo Spas found him in the doorway of his house, which had above it written the date of its construction – 1913 – 'making it the oldest house still inhabited here'. Alekso was the same age as Dedo Spas and greeted us warmly. He had once lived far away in

Malmo for many years but his heart was in the village. His wife was working in the garden, where a vivid array of tomatoes and red peppers were drying on long planks and tables in preparation for the winter sauce-making rituals that take up so much of a Macedonian autumn.

We thanked them politely when they offered to make us another coffee and, after inspecting the huge spreading chestnut tree that Dedo Spas thought was 160 years old, we said goodbye to the old man and his wife and headed back to the house and waited for my wife and son to arrive. Jelena was very hospitable and offered to make us lunch and when my wife finally came we had another coffee and Marco played with the kids, running around the house, though her son was wheezing.

'He has asthma sometimes,' she said. 'I hope it doesn't get worse.'

The outdoor kitchen was a hive of activity as Jelena's grandmother and her friend tended to bubbling pots and chopped fresh vegetables. 'I will try to find that guy,' said Jelena, who was really very eager to help. 'He can come here whenever we ask, Nakolec is not far.'

Dedo Spas had mentioned the man, as old as himself, an Albanian originally from the next village who had emigrated to America long ago. His name was Aslan and when he came it was in an American 4x4. But he was a gentle fellow, not a gangster, and he had a mission. After retiring after 31 years in rock and roll as a nightclub owner near Detroit, he wanted to give something to his native village of Nakolec and was doing so in the form of a Sufi Islamic teke.

'It is basically a monastery,' he said. 'You know, Albania is the headquarters of the Bektashi movement, and in the old days there was always a teke here. So I am rebuilding one, out of marble and stainless steel. There have been three or four documentaries on Albanian TV in Skopje about it,' he said. 'We keep working on it.'

Aslan had been in the army many decades before and wore a baseball cap, and was perhaps even more American than I was. He was also a professional photographer and had a love for the image and I asked for some lessons. He looked at my camera and decided it was good enough, you worked with what you had, and you didn't necessarily need an amazing subject to make a good picture. The light was very important, and so was the angle, and whether the background distracted you from the subject of the composition or complemented it. The lesson was very instructive and we went around the yard practicing on grapes and peppers and empty beer crates with Aslan pointing out what I had done right or wrong.

'Well, that's not too bad, young man,' he said, after we had snapped everything around the house. 'Just keep practicing. Now I had better go home and take a rest. Was very nice to meet you. God bless.'

'And good luck with your teke,' I said.

'He was a nice man,' I said to my wife after Aslan had gone. 'Did you hear any interesting stories?'

'No, I was just relaxing.'

'Does your grandmother have any interesting stories?' I asked Jelena.

'Of course! Just ask her.'

The grandmother was busily preparing lunch and

we went down into the cool stone side room with couches and a table and she was happy to reminisce about the old times when life was very different. She was 81 years old and had had six brothers and sisters. 'We were all sleeping in one room,' she laughed. But life was difficult. During World War I, British military records tell of how mosquitoes killed more soldiers than the enemy on the Macedonian front, further to the east on Lake Dojran, a breeding-ground for malaria. But it was also common to Prespa and I recalled how the man in Plati had told me how a whole village was moved because living too close to the water could be deadly.

'I was married when I was a teenager,' she said. 'Everyone in my "new" family came down with malaria, but I didn't. Neither did my own family.' At the same time, the land was gripped by war, and the Bulgarian fascist occupation. The Germans swept down too to bolster them. 'We tried to escape over the border to Greece,' she said. 'Tito's Partisans came and tried to recruit the men in the villages. They didn't have a choice. Then a Serbian commander came and we heard that his brigade had been destroyed. I went with my child to Montenegro to teach.'

'How did the Germans treat you?' I asked.

She laughed. 'Oh, the Germans were very nice to us.'

'I bet they were,' whispered my wife.

'The girls would sing and dance for the soldiers. Some even got married. But that was before the real fighting began.'

After the war, when the Bulgarians and Germans had been sent packing, the Communists took over but the conservative traditions of the villages remained. She and her late husband were in love for three years, 'but our parents wouldn't let us contact each other,' she said. 'We communicated by secret letters that our trusted friends would bring to us.' It was touching and silly and sweet all at the same time and the old woman was very happy to tell us her stories.

We ate lunch in the cool of the room and then it was time for the children to sleep. 'I don't think we will go to the beach,' said Jelena. 'His breathing is getting worse. But definitely we will do something tonight.'

'All right!' I said. 'We will be in touch.'

We thanked them and headed back to the house where Marco took a nap and I read short stories and drew pictures of the lake from the balcony, a still, sunken mirror between hazy hills. It was utterly placid, and when an editor from London interrupted with a phone call I realized for the first time that I had been away from it all for almost two weeks and had basically no idea what was going on in the rest of the world. It was a rare and wonderful feeling. You lost concentration and peace of mind very fast when there were too many people and computer screens, and I was grateful to the lake and the languor of late summer for preserving me, if even for a few short days, from that intrusive world.

'He's awake,' said my wife. 'If you want, we can go to the beach.'

'Of course we will!'

Chapter 8

We got the red pail and plastic excavation equipment and towels and goggles and so on and set off for the beach. 'What's two kilometres?' I had said. 'In real measurements, it's hardly more than a mile!' Yet mothers never imagined that babies were as tough as you did and she was concerned that we would not make it. 'Of course we will,' I said. 'We have walked places lots of times and we will walk there now. Anyway, the weather is perfect and you have good genes for it.'

My wife's grandparents came from a mountain near Serbia, northeast of the Macedonian city of Kumanovo where she was born. She had told me many stories of how her grandfather would walk 20 miles or so just to get to the town because there was no proper road.

Her other grandfather had been in a Partisan unit in World War II that marched across half of northern Macedonia in close formation. On both sides, if you went back far enough there were Serbian ancestors, as was the case with many in Kumanovo. 'They always said Kumanovo people made good policemen because they were good at beating people,' she had once told me. Didn't I know it!

However, there were no beatings that day, despite the long walk, because it was interesting for Marco and he bumbled along in his yellow hat down the road, which was paved and very straight. A thick belt of trees and reeds kept us from the lake but finally after we had been walking for about 30 minutes, the sand came into view and it was just a question of how we could get down to it.

We found the trail and it suddenly looked very exotic; the beach was all but empty, with a ramshackle cantina near the water and a few palm-frond castaway umbrellas set up. On the right, where the reeds began, one small blue caïque was moored and on the left were the shadowy hills of Greece. The promontory of Psarades jutted out, though the village could not be seen in the dusk, and far opposite us was Albania and the mountain that had so bedevilled George and I on the road to Pustec.

'It's amazing to look at these places where I was before, from here,' I said. 'It's a completely different perspective, like another world – and yet everything is so close.'

'Look at that,' said my wife, pointing to a high white tower to the left. 'That must be for the border police. We are only a few hundred metres from the border, I think.'

I went to test the water and it was surprisingly warm, though of an opacity I had not seen since the Black Sea. 'There are many growing things,' I warned, picking up a brackish green weed and throwing it at my wife, who screamed in panic. 'So I guess you won't go swimming?' I said.

'Too much nature!'

I waded in and the water was warm and surprisingly shallow for a long way out and the weeds were like tentacles, even worse as you could not see them.

I had to swim out a long way and still I would occasionally brush into them. Prespa was a quarter of the depth of Ohrid and, people feared, dwindling each year; rocks that had once been used for diving were now well up above the waterline, and bushes and trees had taken root in long flat stretches that had been underwater until a decade ago or even less. Some believed it was part of a natural cycle affected by the movement of underground plates, which restricted the movement of water into the lake; whatever the truth may have been, one result was the prevalence of flora in the lake, and the birds that came with it.

I floated on my back and listened as a bird would occasionally cry plaintively or dive into the water near the reeds for fish. To float was effortless, compared to Ohrid, because the water was thicker and thicker with life. I looked towards Greece and wondered just where the border was. Did they have some marker buoy? Was there a sign on land? How would you know if you had trespassed across this vital international border? I swam off to find out.

I followed the shoreline and left the beach behind me. To the left was a wild brambly green area and what looked like a small fence that separated it from the beach and I surmised this was the beginning of a no-man's-land before the border. I forged on, but with each stroke in the dark water made even more murky by the gathering dusk, politics invaded my thoughts and I began to think unlikely things, the most outlandish being that there might even be an underwater electric fence ready to zap any would-be economic migrant or other visa-buster trying to break into the Hellenic Republic. It was ridiculous, but disquieting nonetheless and I headed back to the beach, where Marco was making sand-castles and destroying them with his fist.

'How was it?'

'Oh … well, as you said, too much nature. But it was nice and I almost made it to Greece.'

'You're a very dangerous man!' said my wife. 'Are you going to take your son swimming?'

Marco was very happy to finally go in the water and we sat in the calm shallow water twisting the green lakevines on our bodies and throwing rocks.

217

'*Silno*!' he chanted as each one splooshed down into the water. In some ways this lake was much better suited for him than Ohrid. Instead of the rocks or pebbles there, almost all of the shores of Prespa were covered by sand, and since it was shallower the water was warmer too. A two-year-old boy was not in the business of marathon swimming anyway and it was weird and wonderful for him to have these strange green growing things to play with and drape on his mother's head.

'Ugghhh! Get that thing off me!'

Evening approached and the sky, clear with distant clouds over Albania, was reflected on the lake, with pink tones giving way to orange and purple on the rippling surface. The few people had gone and the cantina closed and we set off for the walk home. 'There is still enough light,' I said. 'It won't take that long.'

Nevertheless, before we had got a minute down the road, we noticed an old green military vehicle bouncing over the sand and onto the road. It was the border police patrol on the way back to the village.

'Good evening,' we said. The policeman recognized us from the day before.

'Where do you think you are going now?' he said, with an incredulous grin.

'Well, we were at the beach, and now we are walking home.' I didn't think we had broken any laws.

'At this hour?' he said, shaking his head. 'But don't you know that after sunset, the bear and the wolf come down from the mountain to drink? You had better come with me.'

We were grateful for his help and clambered into the police truck. Marco found it immensely interesting to be in this strange new vehicle with metal bars dividing the back seat from the front and, apparently, no shock-absorbers. As we bounced along down the road, the policemen revealed that the bear was meant to be a gentle bear, but that a gentle wolf was unknown. They did not come all the time, but in any case one should always be careful. The mountain to the east was Pelister, a Macedonian national park. It formed the border with Greece and it was believed that the bears migrated over from the other side of the mountain to escape the Greek hunting season.

Back at the hotel we showered and got ready for dinner but this time Jelena would not be joining us. She said that her son was still sick. We returned to the same restaurant as the night before, and enjoyed another hearty country dinner, before venturing into the village to satiate my love of billiards. There was the table standing outside the shop where the old men passed the time drinking beer and I ordered beers for us and chocolate for Marco. I had developed a fascination for watching British snooker on television, which my wife found mind-numbingly boring, and we played standard American eight-ball. After a couple of games Marco had gotten tired of helping make the shots and wanted to use the cue as some sort of jousting lance and it was time to go.

In the morning I went to look for breakfast in the shop near Jelena's house and her children were on the step, but she was not. I brought some pastries home and my wife called her and thanked her because we would be moving on. We did not see her again but she was very nice and very helpful and said we should come and see her again in Skopje.

There was a bus from the village to Resen at around noon and we were waiting under the tree opposite the school. It was very small and old and I took Marco inside to see it while we were waiting for the bus. Finally the bus came, and we got on along with an old woman from the village. We were going to Pretor, another village 20 minutes along the coast to the north. 'I can drop you down where the village starts,' said the driver, 'but when you go to leave and catch another bus, you will have to walk up the hill to the main road, okay?'

We thanked him for making the detour and the driver pointed out to us the only hotel in the village that was still open. It was the quintessential embodiment of cheerless Yugoslav tourism, with apathetic upholstery and plain wooden drawers and closets. A colony of birds had made nests out of mud on the eaves of the outside balcony and the corner of the bathroom used for showering came with a see-through nozzle. But it was clean and cheap and the moustachioed man at the front desk was friendly. It was the end of the season and we were quite possibly the last guests he would see this year.

'We are looking for Kiril Jonovski,' I said, after we had checked in. The people in Dolno Dupeni had told us that this retired journalist and Pretor local was the expert on the area and it would be worthwhile seeking him out. The desk man brightened at the name and pulled out two books from behind the desk where the keys hung. 'These are his books,' the man said. 'I can sell them to you for 500 denars.'

'Great,' I said. 'But do you know if we can find him?'

He did, and after we had changed our clothes and got ready for the new beach, the man guided us down through a long path through pine trees to where a street passed in front of the beach. He pointed down the street to the left and my wife nodded. 'We will go later, okay,' I said. 'First let's use this warm weather to swim!'

It was another beautiful clear day and the beach was very long and spread before us with the same palm-frond umbrellas and two long piers extending out into the placid water at each end. In the glory days of worker-owned enterprises in the old Yugoslavia, various state-owned companies had special hotels named after them at various points of interest throughout the Federation, at which their employees had special discounted rates. There were also the school field trips from far and wide and the children's camps where vacations could be properly managed.

In the 1960 and 1970s, and even into the 1980s, Pretor and Prespa in general had been a major tourist destination, lauded for its health-enhancing waters, wildlife and fishing. Now, however, it was relatively forgotten, the state-owned hotels shut down or privatized, the school trips from Slovenia or Serbia a distant memory, and even the summer bungalows run-down, with ripped flyers on trees announcing small concerts that had already been held. There was a tinge of sadness to the place but it was still beautiful and not beyond repair.

It was somewhat incongruous, therefore, to come out onto the beach and find an elaborate modern building with tables and a grand terrace, upon which teenage girls in bikinis lay sunbathing on deck chairs. There were two or three small swimming pools and the high-ceilinged building behind it was a modern restaurant and the facing bar glinted with glass and bottles.

'It is a real restaurant,' I reported back. 'Hooray! But let's go to the beach first.'

We went down to the water's edge, establishing ourselves under one of the palm-frond umbrellas. The water was cooler than on the southern side of the lake, but also clearer, and there were fewer weeds. Still, you had to go out a very long way to be in over your head, and farther still to get to a depth where nothing would tangle with your feet, and the people on the shore became specks and disappeared.

Swimming in Prespa was a lonely mission and I didn't know why. I hadn't figured out yet the fatal pull of the lake, its history and its character and its spirit, but I would. Perhaps, I thought, you felt lonely because the lake was small enough that you could see most of it, and there was no place to be alone. It did not offer the anonymity of the sea as did Ohrid. Also its living things were much closer to you than they were there. To the north of Pretor, on the central curve of the lake, lay the Ezerani Bird Sanctuary, and you could hear the birds' cries echoing on the warm air from the heavy reeds far above. It gave shelter to dozens and dozens of different kinds of birds, some of them rare, and you could see them constantly in flight or floating on the water. Although Ohrid also had an abundance of rare plants and animals, they were more subdued, more hidden, whereas shallower Prespa was bursting with them.

I slowly made my way back to the shore and waved from the water at Marco, who recognized me and excitedly waved back. 'Oooh! *Marko ke pliva!*' he shouted, announcing that he would swim. The beach was long and the sand was soft in the water and he could walk in it easily. He splashed the water with big kicks and then we sat in the water and thrashed around for a while, looking for rocks to throw with '*silno*'.

He did not want to get out but we had to, and

after drying off we went up to the restaurant where they had a proper spread and a hungry kitten which tantalized Marco into throwing it cheese on a more or less regular basis. The beer seemed sweeter than usual and the hunter's *pleskavica* delicious and nourishing. There was nothing like eating after having been swimming, when you were cleaned out and stretched out and tired in that vague whole-body way that was only accentuated by beer. I was very happy with how the day had turned out and leafed through the books we had bought.

'Do you think we can find this man?'

'Why not?' my wife answered. 'It would be hard to miss him in a village this small.'

After the food and iced coffee we went back to the beach to watch the afternoon fade and play some more. Marco had been thrown off his usual schedule due to the irregular travel, usually missing his naptimes, but he was enjoying himself too much to care. He did not even know what travel was but knew that he liked going places and he was happy with the simple things we could provide. Nature provided the rest and the birds and seaweed and water kept him engrossed and on the move. 'We are very lucky to have such a perfect son,' I said to my wife.

'I thank God every day for that.'

Evening was approaching and the sun was sinking over Mount Galicica on the western shore when we left the beach. We walked along the beach road where the signs of old Yugoslavia lingered, the overgrown bungalows and rusted signs proclaiming the leisure property of this or that public enterprise. There were very small shops built of rusted metal in various bright colours, all in a row and all shut. Set back from the beach in the trees was a large rectangular hotel for students which looked as if it itself had graduated.

'This is incredible,' I said. 'It is like a ghost town.'

'It is a shame what happened to my country,' said my wife. 'I don't know was it because they fuck up something in Yugoslavia or it's just modern Macedonia "moving forward". But it's really a disaster.'

She had been from one of the last generations of Tito's 'Pioneers', the name given to elementary school students who would wear blue-and-white uniforms with the blue Partisan cap and the Yugoslav red star on it and salute the President-for-Life at the beginning of the school year and on his birthday, even long after he was dead.

'Yes,' she laughed, 'we had many sayings we had to repeat, like "*i po Tito, Tito*" – that is, "and after Tito, Tito". Or, "*druze Tito, mi ti se kunemo*" – "Comrade Tito, we swear to you". It was very funny.'

'What else did they have you do?'

'There were some special events like the carrying of the torch of unity, from Slovenia through all the Yugoslav republics, all the way to Gevgelija in the bottom of Macedonia. I remember, I was so nervous when I got to carry the torch –'

'You got to carry it? How old were you?'

'I don't know, eight or ten,' she said. 'I remember being so nervous, I was running with it from my school about half a kilometre to give it to someone else. I was so afraid – what if it went out or I dropped it? I don't know when they stopped that. But I remember that the year above us in school were the last ones to go on the full excursion around Yugoslavia. We were supposed to go but then the war started in Slovenia. We only got to go to Macedonia and Serbia. We were so sad.'

The bygone beauty of Pretor seemed to mirror her melancholy. It was not only in Macedonia where Yugo-nostalgia held a certain sway among people who recalled a time when they had a secure job and health care and vacations and things were more or less fair.

For me it was fascinating from another point of view. 'Today people in the West are unhappy because they have too many choices,' I said. 'And now after Communism the people here are falling into the same trap. You see? Every year they are less and less happy. They just want more things.'

'Oh, you're just saying that because we don't have anything,' she snapped. 'I'm sure if we had money you would be very happy to buy things too.'

'You are just bitter because Tito didn't let you have enough words!' I said. I had a peculiar theory that the lack of certain basic words in Macedonian was probably due to a socialist conservation programme dictated by the Chairman. But I could not prove it.

'Oh shut up!'

Next to the last set of former state-owned factory vacation villas stood a gated house with a very large lawn and a dog barking inside. Kiril Jonovski was in his blue gardening clothes and pushing the lawnmower and he didn't hear us at first because of that. He was balding and had very large glasses and was very friendly. He invited us to sit on the patio among the flowers and brought butterscotch candies for Marco, who shyly said thank you and unwrapped the candies in secret.

Kiril was a Prespa original, born and raised in Pretor, and a retired journalist for Radio Television Skopje. He was from one of the oldest families in the area and spoke reverentially of a scroll that traced his forebears to the court of Tsar Samuel. Kiril had presided over a society for the protection of Golem Grad island on the other side of the lake and a committee for the beautification of Prespa, among other things, along the way conducting detailed historical research for his books and articles.

We asked him about what had happened, with

all of the closed hotels and decrepit former worker's collectives.

'Up until the 1980s, we would have over 50,000 people a year coming here for vacation,' he lamented. 'So many students would come here from all over Yugoslavia!' He showed us black-and-white photos of masses of vacationers swimming, water-skiing or lounging on the beach, something that seemed so improbable to us but which had obviously happened.

'Pretor itself was a Roman town,' said Kiril, 'as you can tell from the Latin name – the title of a Roman army commander [*praetor*]. It was near the Via Egnatia, and we have found remains of Roman villas and necropolises. But the most unusual thing,' he continued, 'is a very rare tile that was found here, created for the cult of the Anatolian goddess Ma, from Cappadocia. It is only the third such tile found in the world.'

'Really!' I said. There were many questions I had for him but he told us that many interesting things were in his book. Snowstorms and cold froze and blanketed the lakes in the year 927. Even the chroniclers of the day noted it, giving the lake its name:

231

the old Slavic word *prespa*, meaning 'snowdrifts', came into use to describe the place.

'These villages and their names, most of them go back to those times and they are mentioned in the medieval records,' he said. 'This is a very old and important place – you know that Tsar Samuel based his empire on the island of Sveti Achil in lower Prespa. And the remains of the Constantion Fortress, where the Byzantine Emperor Basil II created to subjugate him in 1018, are found north of the lake, near the village of Bolno.'

'What about the more recent history of how the lake got to be so divided, between the three countries?' I asked.

'Oh, that is a complicated story of the wars and occupations and the different interests of Greece and Bulgaria and Serbia, and the Great Powers,' he said. 'But I will tell you one story that is not in the book.'

'Please,' I said.

'A long time ago I was talking to a very old man in Resen. He told me that he when he was a boy, after the war, the Great Powers sent a committee that would go around the lake and decide how to divide it up. He said he was driving carriages for some of these emissaries. And you know what they did?'

'What?'

'To make their report, they needed to find out about the locals. But they were clever. In every village they went to along the lake, they would toss silver coins in the air – but only in front of the children, because the children never pretended; they would always start shouting and run up when they saw the money. The point was to find out what language the children were naturally speaking in each village. They went all around Prespa, and in each of the villages it was Macedonian.'

'But that is not how they made their decision, I guess.'

'Well, that is politics,' laughed the old man.

There were many other things to hear but the most interesting was about the snakes and the mongoose. 'You really must go to see Golem Grad,' said Kiril. 'I know,' I replied. 'Many people have told me that.'

Golem Grad, which in Macedonian literally means 'Big City', was a small island in the southwestern part of the lake, Macedonia's last territorial possession just above the place where three borders met in the lake. It was uninhabited and a protected natural habitat and it was absolutely infested with snakes.

'In the 1960s, we had 100,000 people a year visiting the island,' recalled Kiril. 'I was president of the society then and we restored an ancient church. We also came up with an idea to control the snakes.'

'What did you do?' asked my wife.

'It was the spring of '67, and we decided to import two mongooses from the Croatian island of Mljet. We were careful to make sure that they were two males so they couldn't breed.'

'Did it work?'

'Oh, yes, they killed many snakes. But then the winter killed them. Golem Grad turned out to be too cold for a mongoose to survive. Now that there are not so many visitors, there are even more snakes. But most of them are not dangerous.'

It was a fantastic idea: unleashing mongooses on Macedonia to eradicate snakes on the country's only island. 'We are planning to go over to that side of the lake tomorrow,' I said. 'The locals should be able to take me out there, yes?'

'Sure,' said Kiril. 'It is definitely worth the trip.'

It was well dark and Marco had eaten too many butterscotch candies and we thanked Kiril for his time and promised to drop in again in the morning after we had had time to read through his book. He bade us farewell at the gate and we headed back to the hotel.

'What a nice man,' said my wife.

'Yes, and he really knows a lot of things about this area. It is even more interesting than I thought.'

We went back to the hotel where only the night watchmen were there, watching football on a small television, and we finally got a hot shower and settled down to read. Finally, after Marco had fallen asleep and Buba too, I turned off the light and lay down. Tomorrow would be a big day.

Chapter 9

We left the bags at the hotel in the morning and went back to see Kiril. Marco chased the cats in the garden and messily made bouquets of flowers for his mother. We heard about so many interesting things and it was a pity we did not have more time to stay or to see the famous church at Kurbinovo nearby. 'They have some of the best frescoes in the Balkans!' Kiril had implored us. But we had to be back home in a few days and thus the other side of Prespa beckoned.

We thanked him for all his stories and coffee and candies and he promised to visit sometime when he came to Skopje. When we had lugged everything up to the road we waited in a tiny bus shelter until a minivan came and we were off to Resen. It was sunny and I was optimistic about our chances in yet more unknown territory. After having gone to the far southeast of the lake, at Dolno Dupeni, we would now go to the far southwest at Stenje. 'Actually, there is another village after that, Konjsko, but the bus does not go there,' I said.

'We can see what is interesting when we get there.'

In Resen we changed buses at the little station and made our way west along the top of the lake, passing the entrance to the bird sanctuary, and the bus was soon crowded with children coming home from school. Marco was fascinated by them and they thought he was very funny too, passing him around from one to the other. He was very outgoing and this was good, because we could take him anywhere and he was always happy, except for when he was hungry or tired. In other words, he was basically already an adult.

We passed through several small villages and then one we had thought of staying in, Otesevo. It had been famous in the past for camping and there was supposed to be a hotel, but I thought it better to press on. In any case, Otesevo passed by so fast that we did not have time to notice the little there was of it.

Stenje was the last stop. Some of the schoolboys getting off at the village had told us that they knew of accommodation there and so we stayed on the bus after the first stop, at the entrance to the village, until it turned at the end, past a long line of old houses all facing the shore. It was a remarkably large village with remarkably few facilities.

'They want us to stay in this old room,' I said, after the boy had shown me what was on offer. 'But there is no electricity now and their grandparents are stuck in the next room. But they will let us share the kitchen.'

'What options do we have here?' asked my wife.

'I don't know. There is no hotel.'

'But I thought I saw some rooms-to-rent signs at the start of the village when we were on the bus,' she said. 'Maybe we should go back that way?'

The village had only two streets, both running parallel to the water, and we took the one closer to the beach and marched on in the afternoon heat. It was a long walk and along the way we saw the old people hanging peppers and other vegetables outside old houses of old well-worn brick. The beach was long and sandy, but there were tall grasses between the road and the beach, and then caïques lying hull-up or hull-down along the sand. The village was protected by a spit of land to the north, which also made it seem forgotten, and indeed the sense of things falling apart, in some primeval way, intensified here amongst the unkempt dunes and cows grazing on the beach and the silent mountain that framed Stenje from behind.

When we reached the entrance to the village there was a small police station with a police speedboat on a trailer outside. 'Maybe we can find some place to eat,' I said. 'Go ask the police, they always know if there is a restaurant around.'

She went and the man came out of the old building and pointed us across the road and up, where a small eatery was concealed behind a sculpted arbour. There was even a small fountain playing over rocks in a vaguely Oriental style, and we were very happy to sit down out of the sun and relax.

'Oof, that was a lot of walking,' said my wife.

'But we made it. Let's ask the waiter if he knows where we can stay.'

The waiter brought us our drinks and went off somewhere. He returned a few minutes later with a little old man whose pants were pulled up too high above his farmer's boots. Almost immediately he began referring to Marco as a 'tricky character'.

'He has to call his son in Resen to find it if they he can rent the room,' said my wife after he had left. 'It's a second house, and it's up to his son.'

It was better than nothing and we had at least found some shade and some food and our 'tricky character' was not complaining, but ready to eat and a little bit sunburned. I went inside the restaurant to wash my hands but immediately inside to the right was a counter, and behind it both the bar and the open kitchen. You could see the meat sizzling right in front of your eyes and I was very hungry. The chef was friendly and I told him about our trip and my hope of visiting the island. 'You can find a fisherman to take you,' he said. 'Just go back to the center of the village by the beach and ask around.'

As always, we ordered too much food, but it was just too delicious not to enjoy it. It was already afternoon and with such a big lunch and several beers I would not be swimming today. 'I want to sleep,' I said. 'Beer in the afternoon always makes me tired.'

I was woken up pretty quickly, however, by foreign invaders who literally came down upon us from out of the sky – paragliders, coming down from Mount Galicica, swooping in low over the beach, and landing in a cloud of sand. They looked like enormous tropical birds in their shiny multi-coloured suits and they all sat, ten or twelve of them in the end, around a big table and drank beer. They had polarized sunglasses and dyed hair and were very loud and sounded like Croats, though there were some Slovenes and others among them.

I was alone, jotting down my impressions, while my wife had gone with the baby to see the room that had suddenly become available. The old farmer had indeed got hold of his son in Resen and they were ready to offer us a room. In fact, they already had another one in the same building rented to a couple from Skopje. We would have neighbours.

'It is not so bad,' she said. 'We have to share the bathroom but so what. The bed is very big and at least it's a modern bathroom.'

The door to the balcony was open and a gauzelike curtain billowed in. Our neighbours were playing music and they had their swimsuits on the line. 'I think they have children too,' said my wife.

We went down to see the water while it was still afternoon. There were a couple of rowboats pulled up on the sand and Marco wanted to sit in one and rock the sides. He called it a *kajche*, with the Macedonian diminutive taken probably from Turkish, as almost everything in his world was in the diminutive. '*Koj e vo kajche?*' I asked, 'Who is in the little boat?' With satisfaction he whispered that he was: '*Marko e vo kajche.*'

Afterward, when dusk was approaching, a cool breeze blew on the lake and animated the wavelets, which rippled slowly in hypnotic, scintillating black-and-white zebra stripes out and away from us. 'How can you process that?' I murmured. 'What,' asked my wife. I had been talking to myself.

Up behind us the sun was setting between the cleft of two hills. Edward Lear, the English landscape artist, had reportedly described the view of the lake while crossing the mountain from Prespa to Ohrid in 1848 as the most beautiful he had ever seen; the day after, he returned to the one place on Galicica from where Prespa and Ohrid can be seen simultaneously, inspired to capture the scene. Indeed, there was something about this magical lake region that was indefinable and shifting and you could not put your finger on it because it was always different every time you moved, across or up or down, and always revealed something new of itself.

Back in the center of Stenje, when it was dark, the light from a humble but tidy shop partially illuminated an old basketball hoop set up over the pavement and Marco watched the children throwing a deformed football at it. I asked the shopkeeper how

I could arrange a boat to the island and he pointed out a man sitting in half-darkness on the ledge outside. He had a quiet voice but he spoke some English and we made a deal. The going rate was little over 30 euros for a full day trip and it would take an hour and a half to get there – far longer than I thought. 'But we must go early in the morning,' he said. 'The weather here can be unpredictable in the afternoon. I don't like it.'

We agreed on nine o'clock and I was very happy that we did because it would be the finale I had so richly anticipated at the beginning of the trip. A wild, deserted island, populated by snakes and ruined churches, on the invisible border of three nations! It definitely had possibilities.

The moon was no longer completely full, it was beaten down at the top, but I was too full to sleep and so I went for a walk on the high paved road above the restaurant which led to the Albanian border. The road was silent and totally black and there was nothing on it but forests and stars. I wanted to be alone for a change. There was something about this side of

Prespa that was sinister, but I could not identify it and I thought it was something you could only identify alone and with much concentration and, most likely, from in the water.

At five minutes past nine the next morning, I was back in the center where Mende the fisherman was waiting for me in a cowboy hat and smoking a cigarette.

'Good morning,' I said. 'Nice hat.'

'That's my boat,' he pointed down the beach, 'the blue one. I will get the extra motor and we can go.'

The boat had a wooden keel and metal floor and it looked like it could still float. Mende soon returned with the extra motor. 'Do you mind if my niece joins us?' he asked. 'She and her friend would like to see the island.'

'Why not?' I said. The niece, Natasha, had hair dyed bright red and her friend was named Sarah and had dark round eyes and long hair and was visiting her from Portugal. She was enjoying her visit very much and had been to Macedonia in the past when their friendship began. Natasha was talkative and well informed and it seemed like it would be an interesting trip.

Mende was about forty and had worked for a short time in the American Midwest. 'I was friends with all of the negroes,' he revealed. He pointed back at the opposite cape which made up the curve in the bay before Stenje. 'There is Otesevo,' he said. 'I worked there in the hotel for three years, until it burned down.'

With his hat that cast a shadow over his face in the morning sun, dangling cigarette and sure hand on the tiller, the tanned and weathered Mende reminded me of the Marlboro Man from the classic cigarette adverts. I said as much and everyone laughed. 'You're right!' said his niece. 'Thank you very much,' he said.

'We hear that a Portuguese company is investing in Otesèvo,' she said. 'They will build some eco-tourism place, for bird-lovers and also some kind of health spa.'

'Interesting.' There were indeed rich opportunities for birdwatchers. Fluffy down from birds floated everywhere on the water like cotton. 'Look over there!'

247

There was an enormous flock of orange-billed pelicans floating and then flapping up into the blue sky and we rushed to take photos. 'Beautiful,' said Sarah as she tried to catch the birds before they flew out of range.

'Do you know how the pelicans eat?' said Mende.

'Tell me.'

'The cormorants go down, the fish go up, and the pelican just opens his mouth.'

I laughed. 'No, it's true,' he said. 'A pelican needs twelve kilos of fish every day. So you can see, we have many pelicans, so many fish too.'

'What are the biggest fish in this lake?'

'The carp can get very big,' he said. 'Twenty-five, thirty kilos.'

We passed along the coast, going slowly to see the details, which kept curving in and folding upon themselves with white rocks and dead gnarled trees and small bushes between the rocks. 'I remember when I was a teenager, all of that used to be water,' lamented Natasha. 'We used to swim there and dive off that big rock.'

'Why is the water so dark?' I asked.

'It's a mystery. You know, for the last ten years, no one has done any research. Why is it so dark? Why is there so much algae now? The waters are receding, but nobody is doing anything about it. And the farmers have to stop using the lake water for irrigation.'

'And the littering isn't helpful either,' I said. 'That is a problem.'

Sarah's dark eyes lit up. 'If I tried that in Portugal, they would arrest me!'

'Yes, but that is the EU,' said Natasha. 'People here have to change their whole mentality about things.'

It was a glorious day to be on the lake, the sun glinting on the unbroken surface of blue and not a cloud in the sky; the skipper's concern about bad weather seemed incongruous to me. But the lakes of Macedonia were always unpredictable.

We passed a long sandy spit of land extending into the water and the island came into view, round and thickly set and with an indescribable menace as it seemed to expand and contract slowly in the hot haze. On the inside of the sandbar was Konjsko. It was a tiny village of only a few houses and the road connecting it with Stenje was rugged and rocky.

'How many people live there?' I asked.

'The last full-time resident, an old man, died two years ago,' said Natasha.

'So no one lives there?'

'There are only summer houses,' she said. 'People from Skopje or who used to live in the area and come from elsewhere.'

'It's an idyllic location,' I said. 'Completely sheltered and all on its own away from anything.'

A wooded cliff separated it from Stenje to the north, but to the south Konjsko was also isolated by a barren rock face that stretched in a bleak straight line down the coast. 'No man's land,' said Mende. 'That is where the border with Albania begins.'

I told them about my time in Pustec and what the people there had said about their life and the difficulties the borders caused them. We kept chugging down the lake, getting closer to the island and a small glint of civilization appeared on the other side of the cliff. 'That is Globocani,' he said. 'The first

Macedonian village in Albania. Very small.' Coming from the other side, from Greece, it had been not the first village but the last, too remote to consider. The shifting perception of the same places made possible by the water, which I had noticed throughout the trip, became still more surreal seeing it.

Golem Grad loomed out of the haze as we got closer and it started to look like a fat green cake, perhaps of some organic drug. The maddening refraction of it against the water and sky continued until we got close enough to see the details and then it became an astonishing phantom of bleached white bones, fantastic, brittle trees out of which a hundred black-winged birds flew and the base of it was huge smooth white rocks like sharp cubes in a painting made long ago by a absinthe-drinking Surrealist.

'Incredible,' I said.

'It is white because of the guano,' said Natasha. 'Since it is a protected area, so many birds live there.'

We came around the corner and the Marlboro Man pointed to a tiny aperture in the rock where a painted cross with flowery ends and an inscription in Glagolitic, the precursor of Cyrillic, lay hidden. 'It is very old,' said Natasha. 'Maybe the oldest in Prespa. From the time of St. Clement of Ohrid in the 9th century. There is also a cave where the Ilinden revolutionaries hid their weapons in 1903,' she added.

The skipper slowed the motor and we started to turn towards the place where we would land. 'Will we find a lot of snakes?' I asked.

'I don't know,' she said. 'There are many more in the spring. We are used to it. But I came here in April with some friends, and when we pulled up, the whole ground moved away – it was all snakes sliding into the brush away from us. That was too much. We just turned back without getting out!'

'Amazing,' I said. I told them about my visit with Kiril and the Croatian mongoose project. 'Obviously they can't get rid of them,' I said, 'so why not just go full-on with it? You could import King Cobras and pythons – it would be like a snake theme park!'

They laughed. 'Yes, the tourists would love that,' said the Marlboro Man.

We came around the side of the island where there was a small rocky cove and jumped out. There was a huge whooshing sound from the undergrowth. 'Those are the snakes greeting us,' grinned Natasha. It was for real.

Mende waved us off and started to cruise around to the other side of the island, which was surprisingly big and high, and wait for us there where the proper landing place was. I don't know why they had decided not to land us there, for here there was just a slanted cliff of dust and dirt and scrub which we had to carefully scramble up sideways. I had no boots, only open sandals with black socks, but the nettles and rocks were the least of my worries. When we got to the top, out of breath, I finally asked.

'So really, are any of these snakes dangerous?'

'Most of them are not,' said Natasha. 'But the very small black ones are poisonous. They go very fast and sometimes you can find them under rocks. So you should watch your step and try not to disturb any rocks or logs.'

That was easier said than done on this barren

island that was like a cross between Texas and Mars. But more elegant signs of life soon appeared in the form of a slanting plastered stone wall that lined the lake shore far below. Inside it were small chambers and other walls. It was the ruins of a medieval church, and once again it seemed that the Orthodox monks had known just where to build to get the spectacular effect of aesthetics and nature.

'Wow,' I said. 'This is beautiful! So there were people living here?' I asked.

'Oh yes. Churches were built at least from the 4th century, and people lived here until the 15th or 16th century. One of these compartments was probably a reservoir.'

It seemed impossible to imagine human life in such a bizarre environment. But, I learned, seven churches had existed at one point. 'I imagine there was less of a snake problem in those days?'

'I'd say so,' said Natasha. 'Look at this!' said her friend. There was a dry, husky black-and-white dotted snakeskin. Natasha held it up. 'Look at this,' she said. 'We will see many as the snakes are shedding their skins.'

From the wall of the ruined church the lake was utterly still, with the mountains of Pelister and the opposite shore hazy and indistinct. Somewhere over there lay Dolno Dupeni and Pretor, where I had been so recently, and so continued the game of shifting mirrors made possible by the lake.

Out of the cracks in the unexcavated walls Mediterranean plants and pink and white flowers waved delicately in the breeze. The branches crackled underfoot but it was dark under the trees and there were pine needles to cushion your feet. The feeling of isolation was immense and I wanted to hurry up, but was mindful of Natasha's warning. I did not want to disturb any rocks or logs and chose my steps carefully.

'This clearing here is where we saw the poisonous snake last time,' she informed us as we plodded through the trees, mostly pine. The ground was not covered with white like the cliffs. I sensed that even the birds stayed out of this murky interior.

Eventually we came out on the north side of the island where the forest gave way to the hallucinatory jungle of jagged bones. All of the trees and rocks were bleached white, courtesy of the birds, and where they were clustered they looked like bare skeletons standing out against the blue of the lake.

'It is like Christmas here!' I remarked. 'What amazing photos we can take!'

The friend from Portugal was also keen on photography and we took our time going through this side of the island, with its weird potential and brilliant contrasts of colour. I thought of the tips the Albanian-American photographer in Dolno Dupeni had given me and I was approaching everything from experimental angles. The island eminently deserved some close scrutiny.

It was very hot and we drank some water. 'That is a *foja*,' said Natasha, pointing up at an austere bent tree with curved candelabra branches and thick mops of green soft needles. 'It is very rare and one of the reasons why this island is a protected habitat.' The *foja* was a sort of juniper that was originally from the Caucasus and had somehow spread to this unlikely island in Macedonia. The trees were slow-growing and hardy, some of them being several centuries old.

We reached the edge of the cliff, from where it was a steep drop far down into the water. From crevices in the rocks small green bushes occasionally protruded, with spreading fingers like a pineapple-top, or a wizened tree with bare white branches extended as if in supplication at the moment of death. Everything was weirdly frozen and a hollow carcass of a small fish lay on the rock, a victim of the birds that circled and cried above or swooped with sharp beaks into the blue of the lake.

'This is straight out of Hitchcock,' I said. 'What a place.'

We spent a long time taking pictures from every angle, almost falling down the cliff in the process, and then turned back into the trees until we came out above a small trail where we encountered the first people we had seen – a small family hiking up from the other direction, where the proper landing place was. For the first time there was a discernable path and we started down it in clouds of dust. 'Look,' said Natasha, 'there's a big one!'

It took a long time to make it out because it was

deep inside the tree and blended in well, but then the coils of a very large snake could be seen. 'She's beautiful,' said Natasha. 'She doesn't move at all – she can see us.'

It was the first live snake we had seen, though others had slithered away ahead of us, and it left the eerie feeling that we were being watched from all sides in the thick jungle. Then where the trail bottomed out we came upon a church, but this time not just ruins, and went inside. 'Sveti Petar,' said Natasha. 'From the 14th century.'

It was high and built of stone with a roof of dark red tiles spreading across it. Inside there were candles for sale and worn frescoes on the walls, and even a guest book where the appreciation of many people was written in many languages. It was cool and musty in the church and we stayed there, thankful to be out of the afternoon heat. Some of the frescoes inside were rarely found in the Balkans, as the historian Kiril of Pretor had attested, such as the 'Escape from Egypt' and another depicting a siege of Constantinople, that sumptuous capital which those exiled to these distant

Macedonian lakelands for political or religious reasons could only have dreamt of.

I was always impressed at how, even in the most remote chapels and shrines in the Orthodox world, such as a tiny ruined church far up on the Ohrid coast, someone had always left the candles for sale and the money for them was always left untouched. Just as I had seen once on a ruined chapel ledge on the Ohrid shore, accessible only by boat past Sveti Zaum, the 10-denar notes with the colourful peacocks lay in order like a crumpled fan inside the 14th-century church of Golem Grad, and people respected the custom. We signed the book and went out, down through another wide forest to where another ruined church stood, but only the foundations were visible.

'Come on,' she said, 'he is probably getting bored waiting for us.'

We trudged back up through the pine-needles and around and down to the new coast where sure enough we saw Mende sitting in the sun with his cowboy hat over his face like a sleeping Mexican. 'But we still didn't see as many snakes as I expected,' I said. 'It's not snake season,' said Natasha. 'But let's take a look. These big bushes usually are where they hang out.'

She peered and peered into the darkness of one broad leafy tree and sure enough – 'Take a look at this one!' she called excitedly. It was hard to see at first. 'Use your zoom,' she said, pointing at the camera. That brought the snake, which was shy and coiled up, much closer. It was breathtaking, green and thick with yellow-and-black eyes and a forked tongue pointing at us. It was at least five feet long, coiled and curled around the branches as if part of the tree.

'Amazing,' I said. 'Now that is a snake!'

Our desire for snakes sated, we shoved off from the island. Mende was glad to hear that we had enjoyed it. I asked whether we could continue down a little to the tri-border marker, a mere commemorative buoy in the water. 'Just think about it,' I said. 'I would be in the *Guinness Book of Records* – swimming through three countries in five seconds!'

They thought it was funny but Mende said no. 'The Greek police will come from Nivici with their patrol boat and chase us away. They don't let you get close to the marker.'

Instead we headed back towards Stenje, but this time as close to the Albanian shore as we could without straying beyond Macedonian waters. 'How would you even know?' I questioned. On the rocks in no-man's-land, a faded and rusted Yugoslav sign in Serbian warned of the border. The whole thing made me think again of the silliness of the borders. 'So do you guys know anything about how these borders were agreed on?' I asked, and told them about Kiril's tale of the Committee throwing silver coins in the villages of Prespa. 'I am trying to figure this out.'

'There are different stories,' said Natasha. 'My great-great-grandfathers were all priests. One was sent to Albania, so I have relatives still in Korce. I was told that the Great Powers decided according to whether you lived closer to the three major towns of those days – Korce, Bitola and Thessaloniki. Depending on that they divided the villages.'

'Very strange,' I said, 'but I guess it made sense considering the transportation issues then.'

'But my father heard another story,' she continued. 'A long time ago, a very old man from Konjsko told it to him. When a committee from the Great Powers came in this area, they wanted to give his village to Albania. It was a terrible thought. So what did the man do? They invited the committee into their house in Konjsko, and held a feast in their honour that lasted all night. They gave the Europeans roast lamb and a lot of wine and as they got more drunk, he persuaded them that Konjsko was a Macedonian village and should not be given to Albania. And so it happened.'

'A true patriot,' I concluded. 'Food and drink – that is the Macedonian way.'

'Ha, you are right!'

The water was as smooth as glass and on the sandbar beyond Konjsko some merry middle-aged sunbathers had gathered. They waved to us as we passed by and then we had turned the corner and Stenje was not far. The sun suddenly disappeared behind a cloud and the surface of the water went dark with scattered patches of delicate snowy down. We pulled in at another small beach to visit a church with a mixture of red tiles and some green with moss that towered above on a cliff. A great mass of congealed yellow candles wrapped in newspaper lay outside. From the top the view of the lake was spectacular and the caïque just a tiny dot floating offshore.

Finally we came into Stenje and Marco and Buba were waiting for us. An island full of snakes was no place for her nor, she reckoned, for me either, and she was glad to see me back without snake venom in my veins. But I had saved the brittle snakeskin and flung it at her.

'Yeeek!' she shrieked and we all laughed. I thanked the Marlboro Man for the experience and paid him his due, and we said goodbye to Natasha and her friend and went to have a coffee at a small café above the beach. I told my wife about the trip and then about the sign marking the island as protected in Macedonian, Albanian and the Greek language and that was when the waiter came up.

'A frappé, please.'

She was eager to know about the adventure and

kept asking me questions and looking at the pictures and the waiter brought me something with banana. It was disgusting.

'Ach!' I said. 'I forgot!'

Just a momentary lapse into thinking in Greek had made me forget where I was and my admonition to George: *if you order a frappé in Macedonia, you will not get a real frappé. You will get something disgusting with banana.* Yet only a few kilometres away, across the water, in Greek Macedonia, they would have understood completely differently.

'It is too ironic,' I said.

My wife laughed at me. 'You know what else is funny?' she said. 'Today is the 15th anniversary of Macedonia's independence referendum from Yugoslavia.'

'Is that so,' I said. 'Well there's another fitting reason to have gone to that island then. I bet nobody here even thinks of it when they think of their country. But it really is a whole different world. Amazing.'

I wanted to go swimming, probably for the last time as we would leave the next day. We went down to the beach where other people were sunbathing too. My wife had met a woman of about 50, also from Kumanovo, who had come alone for a week to the lake. She had said she had a problem with her breathing and bathing in the lake waters, so rich in nutrients, was good for her condition. Only much later would we learn that she had come because she was dying of cancer.

The water was dark and I did not want to go in. I was afraid maybe I would not want to come out. The weeds were also thicker than on the other side of the lake but the real issue was the 'snow', that is, the fluffy bird down that clung to the surface. I had to push it away with my hands even as I pushed away the vines with my feet and they slithered off of my chest. Looking behind me I could see that my wake went on for a very long way, like the trail of a shooting star in the night sky, and the bubbles were thick and long-lasting. It was not the ethereal water of Ohrid, that was for sure.

After a while there were no more weeds or feathers and the water was deep but still brackish. I thought again about the two lakes I had seen from every side and swam in over the previous two weeks, and what was it that made them distinct. Every body of water has a unique identity and nature and Ohrid and Prespa were no different. I had already noted Ohrid's indifference, its silence and spirituality and great lucent being; what, then, of Prespa?

For me, it was a story of life and death, of mortality and great fertility. That was the story the lake told. It had a collective memory and it had islands – three of them, Golem Grad, Mal Grad, further down in Albanian waters, and of course St. Achilles in the smaller lake. It had a heritage of empires and great battles and its four banks were all incredibly different. Its dark depths had gathered, as if by magnetism, all the emotion of the dying generations that had come before and that will come after. Unlike Ohrid, which did not care if you sank in its green shafts of light to a cold land of eternal sleep, or perhaps awakening, Prespa longed to pull you down, into its heart of thick confused passions and love and hate and life and death. If Ohrid represented the soul, Prespa represented the body. It was that simple.

I came out of the water and the surface was still disturbed where I had been. My wife and son had been joined by Natasha and her Portuguese friend and Marco was playing in the sand. We sat there and enjoyed the afternoon and then left to go home. We chatted with the people from Skopje, who had brought all of their cutlery and food with them as if heading out on an expedition.

'So many people do that,' my wife said. 'They want to save every denar. Maybe we can learn something from them.'

'I don't care about that,' I said. 'I'm tired. Let's go out.'

We went out to the garden restaurant again and the border policemen were there as usual, yelling at the boy to bring them more beers. 'It must be great to be them,' my wife said. 'They have basically no work to do and can just drink and relax all day.' I laughed. 'It's the same story everywhere.'

The wind had started to pick up and the temperature went down and we decided to sit inside. 'Hey, maybe that fisherman was right,' I said. 'Looks like the weather might get bad. I'm sure glad I went to the island today. That was lucky.'

'You are always lucky,' she said. 'Like I always say, you have a very shiny star.'

We slept heavily and well and when we woke up the sky was grey and the lake, volatile. The old man who had pegged Marco as a nefarious troublemaker told us that the bad weather was likely to last for three days. 'Did you hear that?' I said to my wife. 'If I hadn't gone to Golem Grad yesterday, no chance I would have been able to go. I really was lucky!'

We had a small breakfast and packed our things to make the long trip back to Skopje. We were very tired but had done everything we came to do and more, and the little boy had been heroic in his fortitude and optimism during constant travelling.

'Come, let us go to the beach,' I said.

'No! It's too cold!'

'Oh, come on. The waves are so big!'

We walked down to where the long grass began and the steely grey waves cresting into whitecaps were breaking with great booms on the shore and spitting

268

out pieces of branches. All of the caïques had been drawn up onto the sand and the only boat bobbing in the water was the white police patrol boat at its mooring. On the left where the sand began a large bull sat flicking its tail, seemingly uninterested in the storm.

'Oooh!' murmured Marco. '*Golema voda*!' ('Big water!').

'There is a cow,' I said, pointing to the bull. 'How does a cow talk?'

'Moooo!'

We started to walk down through the grass to the beach and my wife was swearing because we were being lashed by sand and I had to pick Marco up and shield him from it. 'This is the most stupid idea you could have had!' she shouted.

But there was something more stupid. The bull had pricked up his horns and was looking at us with peculiar interest. I turned around, and then I turned around again.

'Look at you!' I said. 'You're all dressed in red!'

My wife indeed had a red dress and shirt on and she gasped. We backed gingerly onto the pavement, continuing down past where the bull was. 'I don't want to go down there!' she protested. 'It's okay, I will take Marco myself. I want to show him the water.'

I picked the little boy up and we walked down through the blowing sand to where the little caïque that he had sat in the day before was pulled up. There was a harsh wind blowing in from the lake, which had been so placid all week, and the waves crashed and sprayed us from a distance. 'Oooh!' said Marco, transfixed. We watched it together.

Then for some reason I thought of a song that was meant to be a sad song but I remembered it from a time of my life which was very happy and very mysterious. There was one line in it that I always remembered:

How did I meet you? I don't know

A messenger sent me in a tropical storm.

I blinked and picked up Marco from where he had decided to get his pants dirty in the sand. We threw some rocks with *silno* into the crashing waves and tried to avoid their spray, but when it hit us anyway he would laugh and laugh.

I pointed to the rowboat in the sand. 'Who was in the little boat yesterday?' I asked him. 'Marco was,' he dutifully responded. It was neither new nor clean but it could be rescued with a little love and attention.

'*Ima nikoj vo kajche?*' I asked him ('Is there anyone in the little boat?')

'*Ne,*' said Marco, '*nema nekoj vo kajche.*' ('There is no one in the little boat').

'That's right,' I smiled and stroked his soft hair. '*Nema nikoj vo kajche.*'

hidden europe

the magazine exploring Europe's special spaces

hidden europe magazine celebrates the art of travel. Join us on our journey to places well beyond the usual tourist trails!

We promise a fresh perspective on well trodden paths, and a cool look at undiscovered corners. Crisp, clear and well informed. Sometimes calculated to make you smile, and always managing to make you think.

hidden europe regularly visits the Balkans, exploring

people

places

cultures

from the Urals to the Azores...

visit us at www.hiddeneurope.co.uk

call us on 0049 30 755 16 128
or e-mail editors@hiddeneurope.co.uk